# Anatomy of
# Vehicle Performance

### Cars, Pick-ups, Vans, SUVs and Motorcycles

by Roland D. Nelson, B.S.M.E

Order this book online at www.trafford.com
or email orders@trafford.com

Most Trafford titles are also available at major online book retailers.

Print information available on the last page.

ISBN: 978-1-4251-2523-3 (s)

*Trafford rev. 10/11/2022*

www.trafford.com

**North America & international**
toll-free: 844-688-6899 (USA & Canada)
fax: 812 355 4082

# Acknowledgements

The following companies or publishers have been used by quoting brief passages for the purpose of review.

*Applied Thermodynamics*
    by V. M. Faires
Bavarian Motor Works (BMW)
BSA Motorcycles
Cadillac Division of GM
*Car & Driver* Magazine
Carl's Cycle Sales of Boise Idaho
Chevrolet Division of GM
Chrysler Corporation
Dodge Division of Chrysler
Drake Engineering (Offenhauser)
*Elementary Fluid Mechanics*
    by John K. Vennard
Ford Motor Company
Ford of Great Britain (Cosworth)
Harley Davidson Motorcycle Co.
Honda Motorcycle Co.

Isuzu Corporation
Jaguar Automobile Co.
Kawasaki Motorcycle Co.
*Machine Design* Magazine
Marks Engineering Handbook
*Motor Trend* Magazine
Motors Manual
Nissan Automobile Co.
Oldsmobile Division of GM
Pontiac Division of GM
Road & Track Magazine
Saleen Mustang Co.
Toyota Automobile Co.
Triumph Motorcycle Co.
Volkswagen Automobile Co.
Ida Nelson—transcriber
LaRay Gates—layout & cover design

# Table of Contents

## Chapter 8: Acceleration Calculations

## Chapter 9: Automatic Transmissions

## Chapter 10: Internal Engine/Accessory Friction

## Chapter 11: Volumetric Efficiency/Fuel Consumption

## Chapter 12: Gross Horsepower and Torque Correction—Prior To 1973

## Chapter 13: Shortcut Procedures for Performance Specifications

## Chapter 14: Summary—Beware of Pitfalls

## Chapter 15: Reciprocating Weight

## Chapter 16: Horsepower RPM Formula

## Chapter 17: Torque RPM Formula

## Chapter 18: Calculation Discrepancies 81

## Chapter 19: Torque Drop 87

## Chapter 20:  High Altitude Compensation

## Chapter 21: Effects of Fuel on Torque and Horsepower

## Chapter 22: Turbocharger Effects on Torque and Horsepower

## Chapter 23: Engine Life

## Appendix One: #1 Test Vehicle

## Appendix 2: #2 Test Vehicle

## Appendix 3: #3 Test Vehicle

## Appendix 4:

# Preface

1985 marked the 100th anniversary of the invention of the internal combustion engine by Karl Benz.[1] Since then and on into the 21st century continual revisions, modifications, and additions have been made to the engines and transmissions of production automobiles.

Comments on all of the changes made since 1885 would be virtually impossible; instead, a brief review of the table of contents for this book will show the various basics being addressed. At the time of printing, there was no known publication that covers all the factors that contribute to vehicle performance. This book is intended as a complete package that will allow the reader to study and analyze a vehicle or vehicles to determine with preciseness their specifications and assess them accordingly.

Several complete analyses of vehicles have been included for reference and study in Appendices 1 through 3: #1 Test Vehicle, #2 Test Vehicle, and #3 Test Vehicle. All phases of the analyses are discussed and explained in detail. From these basic studies, a complete analysis of any desired vehicle can usually be made.

---

1 *Colombia Encyclopedia* ©1978, 1979.

# Chapter 1: Introduction

## The "How To" Book

This publication is geared toward car enthusiasts with no more than a high school math education including algebra. Algebraic equations such as "The area of a circle equals pi (3.1416) times the radius squared" or "$\pi r^2$" are given. More complicated formulas are derived from these basic ones and presented in their simplest forms with examples of how the formulas are calculated.

## Data for Selecting or Purchasing a Vehicle

The various car magazines—"*Road & Track*," "*Motor Trend*," and "*Car & Driver*," to mention a few—publish several road tests of various vehicles each month. If you miss the monthly test, you can obtain a copy by writing to the magazine or checking its website. For many buyers, these test reports are sufficient to select a car for lease or purchase.

## Performance Data Obtained from Vehicle Analysis—data not included in magazine tests

- True top speed with a lone driver in the gear used
- Top speed with passengers and luggage
- Hill climbing with passengers and luggage in the appropriate gear
- Fuel economy at highway speeds with passengers and luggage
- High altitude performance

- Trailer towing performance—hill climbing and fuel mileage
- Optimum shift points for hill climbing or dragging
- True torque and horsepower

## Scope of Performance Data

Less than one half the data used in a magazine test report is needed for performance analysis. The data listed in Chapter 2 can be used for guidelines of the actual data required. From this data, the items previously listed can be calculated using instructions given later in this book. The following additional performance data can be calculated:

- Fuel economy with lone driver
- Acceleration at 30 MPH in tall (appropriate) gear (This value gives the driver the type of engine response to the throttle movement.)
- Recommended cruising velocities
- Passing capabilities from 50 to 80 MPH in feet

# Chapter 2:

# Data Required for Performance Evaluation

## Preliminary Research

There are some preliminary data required in order to evaluate vehicle performance. The data that includes various specifications for the specific vehicle can most easily be found in a test report published in a magazine. If a test report is not available, a trip to the library or search on the internet should be made to gather the required data as listed.

## Engine Specs

- Bore—inches (in) or millimeters (mm)
- Stroke—in or mm
- Number of cylinders
- Displacement—in$^3$ (can be calculated from above data)
- Power—HP at RPM
- Torque—lb-ft at RPM
- Compression ratio
- Redline RPM (if available)

## Transmission Specs

- Final drive ratio
- All forward gear ratios[1]
- Torque converter ratio—for automatic transmission[2]
- Transfer case ratio—for automatic transmission[3]

## Tire Data

- Manufacturer's designation (e.g. P195/70-R14)

## Vehicle

- Curb weight in pounds (lbs) *(Note: Curb weight includes all necessary fluids and one-half tank of gas, but no passengers or cargo. Shipping weight does not include fluids.)*

## Performance Specs (if available)

- Velocity and RPM where transmission is shifted: 1-2, 2-3, 3-4, 4-5, 5-6
- Acceleration Times (in seconds):

| | |
|---|---|
| 0-30 mph | 0-70 mph |
| 0-40 mph | 0-80 mph |
| 0-50 mph | 0-80 mph |
| 0-60 mph | 0-100 mph |

- Quarter mile—elapsed time and terminal velocity
- Top speed—MPH

## Trailer Specs

- Weight of trailer—in lbs
- Type and designation on tires

---

1   *Early GM Hydra-matic transmission ratios were in Motors Manual.*

2   *Torque converter ratios were often available from the dealers' brochure. If not available use 2.0 (Avg of 1.667 to 2.35)*

3   *In the 1980s, GM used a 1.12 transfer ratio & a 2.84 final drive ratio, which gave a 3.18 effective final ratio*

# Chapter 3: Engine Performance— Torque and Power

## Preliminary Research

The normal information given in the numerous publications investigated regarding engine performance was the maximum torque with the associated RPM, and the maximum power with associated RPM. However, when a graph was given for the torque and horsepower values through the entire RPM range, the scale was too small to remove accurate data from the graph. This chapter will help you determine the maximum torque (and maximum power) of your automobile at *any* RPM. It contains many equations; refer to Appendix 4: Symbol Definitions to find the meaning of any symbols you are unsure about.

## Horsepower Produced by Torque

The physics definition of power is the rate of producing work. Work, measured in foot-pounds, is defined as the force (in pounds) exerted on an object times the distance (in feet) moved: Work = force x distance. So power is simply work divided by time: Power = (force x distance) ÷ time. Thus a horse could carry a rider one quarter-mile at a trot or at a gallop using the same amount of work, but if the gallop was twice as fast as the trot, the trip would require twice as much power. The unit of power for dealing with vehicle performance is the "horsepower," (HP) defined as 550 *foot-pounds per second* or 33,000 *foot-*

*pounds per minute.* Thus it would take a vehicle with power of 1 HP one second to move 550 pounds one foot. These figures are good for linear motion, but inadequate for rotational motion.

Torque, or work produced in rotation around an axis, is measured by multiplying the applied force (in pounds) by the distance from the axis, that is, the length of the lever arm (in feet). It is measured in *pound-feet* (lb-ft). A wheel with a radius of 1 foot would produce a distance moved (in feet) equal to its circumference ($2\pi r \approx 6.2832$), with each revolution. Multiplying by the number (N) of RPMs will give you feet per minute, and dividing by 33,000 will give the horsepower[1], assuming a wheel radius of 1 foot.

$$\text{Thus, HP} = \frac{T \times 2\pi r \times N}{33000} = \frac{T \times 6.02832 \times N}{33000} = \frac{T \times N}{5252}$$

$$\text{In another form: } T = \frac{HP \times 5252}{N}$$

Thus, when the wheel radius, HP, and RPM are known, the torque can be calculated.

## Torque Between the Maximum Torque RPM and the Maximum Power RPM

Figure 1 on the following page shows the torque and HP data for #1 Test Vehicle. The maximum torque is 44.1 lb-ft at 7,000 RPM. The maximum HP is 65 at 8,000 RPM. Using the formula from section 2 above, the torque at 8,000 RPM is:

$$\frac{65 \times 5252}{8000} = 42.6725 \text{ lb-ft}$$

---

1  *A TI-30SLR scientific calculator or equivalent will perform all necessary calculations.*

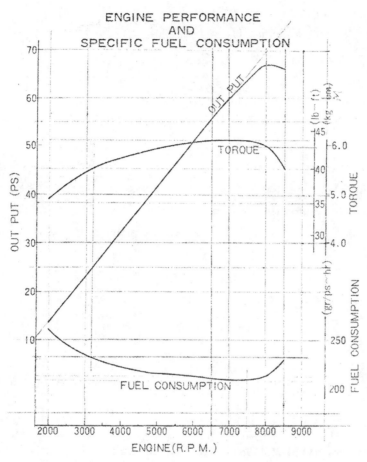

Figure 1

This number is 1.4275 lb-ft down from the peak torque of 44.1. Dynamometer studies have shown that the decrease in torque from the maximum varies as the square of the RPM difference from the maximum torque RPM. Mathematically, the torque at 7,900 RPM is calculated as follows:

$$T = \frac{\lceil 1.4275 \times (79 - 70)^2 \rfloor}{(80-70)^2} - 44.1 = 42.9437 \text{ lb-ft at 7900 RPM.}$$

Note that the RPMs are given in hundreds; i.e., 8,000 RPM is 80 hundred RPM. This was done to prevent various hand and desk calculators from "dropping" digits and giving incorrect calculations.

The calculations of HP at 7900 RPM are as follows:

$$HP = \frac{42.94 \times 79.0}{52.52} = 64.59547 \text{ HP}$$

If the calculated HP at 100 RPM below the maximum HP RPM is over 65, an alternate formula must be used. An example will be given in the section, Torque Between the Maximum Torque RPM and Maximum Power RPM—Alternate, found in this chapter. At the top of page 114 of the #1 Test Vehicle analysis, the $>N_T$ (greater than the maximum torque RPM) is given as 0.014275 (T). The value of the torque drop (see chapter 19) is from 44.1 to 42.6725 (1.4275 divided by $(80-70)^2$ or $10^2$). The "T" shows that the standard formula was used.

Thus, the torque for any RPM, such as 7,521 RPM at 110 MPH in 5th gear, can be found rapidly as follows:

75.21 – 70 = 5.21

$5.21^2 = 27.1441$

27.1441 x .014275 = 0.3875

0.3875 – 44.1 = 43.713 lb-ft, as given in column 3 of page 114 under "T" for torque.

## Torque Below the Maximum Torque RPM

Examination of the HP curve in Figure 1 (on the previous page) shows that the power curve is headed toward a stall or idle RPM as the RPM is reduced. Dynamometer studies have shown that the stall RPM varies with the individual cylinder displacement of the engine. Since the HP reduction is proportional to the square of the RPM difference from the maximum torque RPM, a large error at the stall RPM is very small above 2,000 RPM. As a result, the following stall RPMs have been used.

| Displacement of one cylinder (in³) | Stall RPM (Nᵢ) |
|---|---|
| 35.000 and up | 400 |
| 25.000 to 34.999 | 500 |
| 20.000 to 24.999 | 600 |
| 15.000 to 19.999 | 700 |
| 10.000 to 14.999 | 800 |
| 7.500 to 9.999 | 900 |
| 5.000 to 7.499 | 1000 |

The one-cylinder displacement of #1 Test Vehicle is:

$$\frac{\pi}{4} B^2 S = 0.7854 \times (2.402)^2 \times 2.480 = 11.238 \text{ in}^3$$

From the above table, $N_I$ = 800 RPM. The power at 3,000 RPM is calculated as follows:

$$\text{Power} = \frac{44.1 \times 30}{52.52} - \left[ \frac{44.1 \times 8}{52.52/(70-8)^2} \times (70-30)^2 \right]$$

Power = 22.3944 HP; Torque = 39.205 lb-ft

All calculations in this RPM range are done in a similar fashion. *(Note: RPM is given in hundreds for the reasons given earlier in this chapter.)* At the top of page 114 of the #1 Test Vehicle analysis, the $<N_T$ (less than the maximum torque RPM) is given as 0.0017475. This value is the HP loss at $N_I$, or 800 RPM, and can be calculated thus:

$$\frac{44.1 \times 8}{52.52} = 6.7174$$

$$\frac{6.7174}{(70-8)^2} = 0.0017475$$

Thus, the power for any RPM, such as 4549 RPM at 25 MPH in $1^{st}$ gear, can be rapidly found as follows:

$70 - 45.49 = 24.51$

$24.51^2 = 600.7401$

$600.7401 \times 0.0017475 = 1.0497933$

$$1.0497933 - \frac{(44.1 \times 45.49)}{52.52} = 37.147255 \text{ HP}$$

Convert to torque by multiplying

$$37.147255 \times \frac{52.52}{45.49} = 42.888 \text{ lb-ft}$$

as given in column 3 under "T" for torque.

## Torque Above the Maximum Power RPM

Dynamometer studies of the HP above the maximum HP RPM show that the HP drops in proportion to the square of the RPM difference from the maximum HP RPM. From this information, a theoretical RPM can be calculated that would indicate the RPM where the power has dropped to zero. Although this condition is <u>not</u> feasible, this theoretical "No-load" RPM ($N_L$) has been used to simplify calculations in subject RPM range.

The No-Load RPM ($N_L$) for #1 Test Vehicle is calculated as follows:

$$\sqrt{N_p} \times 0.0625 + 1 = \sqrt{80} \times 0.0625 + 1 = 1.559017$$

$1.559017 \times 80 = 124.72 \text{ RPM}$

$$\text{The power at 8500 RPM} = \frac{65 \times (85\text{-}80)^2}{(124.72 - 80)^2} = 0.8125$$

$0.8125 - 65 = 64.187 \text{ HP}$

$\text{Torque} = 39.660 \text{ lb-ft}$

All calculations in this RPM range are done in a similar fashion. *(Note: RPM given in hundreds for the reason given earlier in this chapter.)*

At the top of page 114 of the #1 Test Vehicle analysis, the $N_p$ (greater than the maximum power RPM) is given as 0.032502. This power is the maximum power loss: 65 HP $\div$ $(N_L - N_p)$ = 65 HP $\div$ $(124.72 - 80)^2$ = 0.032502

Thus the power for any RPM, such as 8,382 RPM at 105 MPH in 4th gear, can be rapidly found as follows:

83.82 – 80 = 3.82

$3.82^2$ = 14.5924

14.5924 x 0.032502 = 0.47428

0.47428 – 65 = 64.5257 HP

Convert to torque by multiplying

$64.5257 \times \dfrac{52.52}{83.82} = 40.431$ lb-ft

as given in Column 3 under "T" for torque.

Some relatively low performance or mildly tuned engines will have higher No-Load RPMs than those calculated. If acceleration times from the test are faster than those calculated, a false, higher HP RPM can be used to find a higher No-Load RPM. Acceleration times can be recalculated until they closely match the test data.

## Torque Between the Maximum Torque RPM and Maximum Power RPM—Alternate

The engine in #3 Test Vehicle has maximum torque of 245 lb-ft at 2,900 RPM; Maximum HP is 170 at 4,600 RPM. Torque at 4,600 RPM is 194.096 lb-ft. Using the standard formula described earlier in this chapter:

$$\frac{245 - 194.096 \times (45 - 29)^2 - 245 = 199.908 \text{ lb-ft at 4500 RPM}}{(46\text{-}29)^2}$$

HP = 171.285

This value exceeds the 170 maximum HP specified. The revised power formula is used as follows:

$$\frac{245 \times 29 - 170 = 34.718203}{52.52}$$

$$\frac{[34.718203 \times (46 - 45)^2] - 170 = 169.880 \text{ HP at 4500 RPM}}{(46 - 29)^2}$$

Torque = 198.269 lb-ft at 4500 RPM

Power at 3000 RPM = $(46 - 30)^2 \times \dfrac{34.718203}{(46 - 29)^2}$ = 30.75384

30.75384 − 170 = 139.246 HP at 3000 RPM

Torque = 243.774 lb-ft at 3000 RPM

This and the previous formula are the only formulas required for this RPM range.

## Turbocharged Engines—Gasoline Fuel

Turbo charged engines are treated the same as normally aspirated engines covered earlier in this chapter. The only exception is if the torque is at a maximum for many RPMs, e.g., the Dodge Shelby Lancer has maximum torque from 3,000 to 4,000 RPM.

## Miscellaneous Engines

The formulas covered earlier in this chapter apply to 4-stroke, 4-cycle piston engines only!

- The formulas are not applicable to 2-stroke, 2-cycle engines.
- The formulas are not applicable to Wankel rotary engines.

# Chapter 4: Rolling Resistance

## Preliminary Research

The only pertinent articles found in the libraries on this subject were in engineering handbooks. The graphic data showed variations in rolling forces in excess of 50% from 0 to 15 MPH. The variation was less between 15 and 30 MPH. Forces were relatively stable (± 5%) above 50 MPH. However, all data pertained to multiple wheel trucks (18-wheelers) under heavy cargo loads. None of this data appeared applicable to passenger automobiles or motorcycles. Due to this situation the research was abandoned.

## Early Measurements

A motorcycle and rider with gross vehicle weight of 450 lbs were pulled with a force (fish) scale and rope to determine the rolling force. A force of 8.0 to 18.0 lbs was measured on smooth level cement and smooth level asphalt in both directions to get a precise average. The 10-pound variation was never determined—it was assumed to be ± 5 lbs (or slightly over ± 0.01 "G"). The nominal of 13.0 lbs used was very close to the 0.029 coefficient, which was later proven correct.

## Tests for Measuring Rolling Resistance.

Since the "fish" scale measurements used earlier were inaccurate for larger vehicles, a new test was needed. Towing with rope and cable with a large force scale seemed cumbersome and inaccurate. So, lacking a better approach, the search was on for a relatively long (½ mile), flat, smooth, level road with minimum wind velocity, for testing. It became apparent that using a calibrated speedometer on such a road and measuring the time to decelerate from one velocity to the next lower velocity, using the gross vehicle weight, would enable the calculation of the rolling resistance. An example of this calculation is given in the section below. Several tests of motorcycles and cars with bias ply tires revealed that the rolling force in lbs was 2.9% of the gross vehicle weight. Further testing of cars with steel radial ply tires revealed that the rolling force in lbs was 2.5% of the gross vehicle weight.

## Test Data for #2 Test Vehicle

### Deceleration Test

| Velocity (mph) | $F_A$ (lbs) | $F_N$ (lbs) | t (sec) | t (sec) (combined intervals) |
|:---:|:---:|:---:|:---:|:---:|
| 40 | 34.52 | 107.31 | — | |
| 35 | 26.43 | 99.22 | 5.540 | 11.517 |
| 30 | 19.42 | 92.21 | 5.977 | |
| 25 | 13.48 | 86.27 | 6.410 | 13.233 |
| 20 | 8.63 | 81.42 | 6.823 | |
| 15 | 4.85 | 77.64 | 7.193 | 14.601 |
| 10 | 2.16 | 74.95 | 7.498 | |

Total Time: 39.441 seconds

$F_A$ = 215.74 lbs @ 100 MPH

$WT_T$ (test) = 2510 lbs

$F_A$ = 72.79 lbs (.029)

The air drag data was generated by using the procedure given in Chapter 8, Calculating Aerodynamic Drag; also, the calculation for #2 Test Vehicle is given on page 118.

The deceleration times are calculated exactly like the acceleration times as shown in Chapter 8, Acceleration Through the Gears.

# Chapter 5: Air Drag

## Preliminary Research

In the first group of performance studies, the aerodynamic drag was the least known factor. At top speed, only four major forces are in effect. Using an accurate estimate of engine force, drive train loss, and rolling resistance, the air drag force (in pounds) can be calculated. This calculated force only holds true for the velocity at which it was calculated.

## Aerodynamic Force Equation

From *Elementary Fluid Mechanics* by John K. Vennard is the following equation:

$$F_A = C_D A_F \frac{\rho V^2}{2G}$$

$F_A$ = Air drag (lbs)

$C_D$ = drag coefficient (no unit)

$A_F$ = Maximum frontal area (ft$^2$)

$\rho$ = air density (lbs/ft$^3$)

$V$ = air velocity (ft/sec)

$G$ = Gravitational acceleration (32.174 ft/sec$^2$)

Thus the aerodynamic drag (in lbs) is proportional to the square of the vehicle velocity.

## Tests for Measuring Air Drag

Using a long (½ mile), flat, smooth, level road with minimum wind velocity, and a calibrated speedometer, measuring the time to decelerate from one velocity to the next lower velocity will enable the calculation of the combined air drag and rolling resistance. Tests with a manual transmission vehicle should be made with the clutch disengaged; with an automatic transmission vehicle, the transmission should be in neutral to eliminate any deceleration by the engine.

## Test Data for #2 Test Vehicle

### Deceleration Test

| Velocity (mph) | $F_A$ (lbs) | $F_N$ (lbs) | t (sec) | t (sec) (combined intervals) |
|:---:|:---:|:---:|:---:|:---:|
| 90 | 174.25 | 247.54 | | |
| 85 | 155.87 | 228.66 | 2.403 | |
| 80 | 138.07 | 210.86 | 2.603 | 5.006 |
| 75 | 121.35 | 194.14 | 2.825 | |
| 70 | 105.71 | 178.50 | 3.070 | 5.895 |

Total Time: 10.901 seconds

$W_T$ (test) = 2510 lbs

$F_R$ = 72.79 lbs (0.029)

t (seconds)

$F_A$ = 215.74 lbs @ 100 MPH

The air drag data was generated by using the procedure given in Chapter 8, Calculating Aerodynamic Drag; also, the calculation for #2 Test Vehicle is given on page 118.

The deceleration times are calculated exactly like the acceleration times as shown in Chapter 8, Acceleration Through the Gears.

## Combined Air Drag and Rolling Resistance

Further studies revealed that the air drag force shown above included a square factor of the rolling resistance. Thus, as the vehicle velocity increased, the rolling resistance slightly increased from the low speed values given in this chapter. Since the values start from zero and progress proportional to the square of the velocity, the values remain as a part of the air drag. The estimated value of this rolling resistance factor is approximately 9% of the low speed value at 100 MPH.

# Chapter 6: Drive Train Loss

## Preliminary Research

All efforts at estimating power loss between the engine and the drive wheels ended with no results whatever.

## Early Measurements

In 1957, the design and fabrication of a motorcycle dynamometer was completed. The power from the engine was transferred through a 0.500-inch pitch primary chain, direct drive transmission (4th gear), and a 0.625-inch pitch final drive chain to the final sprocket—the dynamometer or the rear wheel. Since the engine torque was estimated at 35.0 lb-ft at full power, 35.0 lb-ft of torque with a calibrated torque wrench was applied at the engine sprocket. The opposing torque at the rear (dynamometer) sprocket was measured at 90% of the theoretical torque with a second, higher capacity, calibrated torque wrench. Further tests revealed that the 10% loss was <u>not</u> proportional to the applied torque: it was 10% of the torque at maximum power—a fixed value—throughout the velocity range.

## Various Measurements

Measurements made on several rear-drive cars in direct drive (4th gear) revealed a 20% loss from the engine to the drive wheels. Again, this loss is based on the torque developed by the engine at maximum power.

Front-drive cars with transverse engines revealed a 10% loss with engine oil or equivalent in the transmission; 12% loss is normal when 80 to 90 weight gear lube is used.

Measurements made on several motorcycles in high gear revealed a 10% loss using 0.625-inch pitch rear chain. The loss increased to 11% when a 0.750-inch pitch rear chain was used. These percentages work for all other gear ratios.

Analysis of a shaft drive Honda Gold Wing motorcycle produced a 15% drive train loss associated with the bevel gears used from the shaft to the drive axle.

In-line engines (in which the center line of the crankshaft points at the front of the car) coupled with front-wheel drive, as presently used in some Chrysler products, have an estimated drive train loss of 15% when the transmission ratio is 1/1.

Analysis of the 2004 BMW 530i, a rear-drive car, revealed a drive train loss of less than 12%. The 20% previously given is normal when hypoid pinion and ring gears are used with the center line of the pinion gear offset from the center line of the ring gear. BMW has obviously redesigned the rear differential drive to reduce friction in order to compete with the front-drive cars while preserving the superb handling characteristics of their rear-drive cars.

The loss in any gear other than direct drive (1/1) is directly proportional to the transmission ratio. The estimated value of the loss in pounds can be found by using the Multiplier explained in Chapter 7. The Multiplier is the overall gear ratio divided by the effective radius of the rear wheel in feet.

## Manual Transmissions

For approximate estimates of the drive train loss in each gear for manual transmissions, proceed as follows:

1.  Estimate the drive train loss for the transmission ratio nearest or slightly higher than 1.0. Typically 0.10 is the normal loss for front drive-transverse engines.

2.  For transmission ratios greater than 1.5: add the ratio to the 0.5 power and the ratio to the 0.25 power, and divide by 2. Multiply this number by the ratio in Step 1 to give an approximate drive train loss. The actual loss is the torque value at the maximum power RPM multiplied by the multiplier for the gear used times the number found for this gear. The value is in pounds and is only an approximate value.

3.  For ratios from 1.0 to 1.5, raise the ratio to the 0.5 power and add the direct ratio, then divide by 2. Multiply this number by the ratio in Step 1 to give an approximate drive train loss.

4.  For ratios less than 1.0, raise the ratio to the 0.0625 power and multiply by the ratio in Step 1. These values often cannot be verified with acceleration data and must be used as calculated.

When matching acceleration times with actual test data, it is often necessary to vary the drive train loss to match the actual test times. The obvious reasons for this are (1) oversized gears, (2) a different gear lube, and (3) 3$^{rd}$ gear is often in the center of the transmission and causes higher losses due to shaft deflections.

## Automatic Transmissions

For approximate estimates of the drive train loss in each gear, proceed as follows:

1.  Estimate the drive train loss for the transmission ratio nearest or slightly higher that 1.0. Typically 0.10 is the normal loss for front drive-transverse engines.

2.  For transmission ratios of 1.0 and up, subtract 1.0 from the ratio and multiply by 0.035. Add this value to the value found in Step 1.

3.  For transmission ratios of less than 1.0, take the reciprocal (1 over the ratio), subtract 1.0 from the ratio and multiply by 0.035. Add this value to the value found in Step 1. These values often cannot be verified with acceleration data and must be used as calculated.

## $F_D$ in Top Gear

If top speed is achieved in a gear at an RPM less than maximum HP RPM, the $F_D$ is the appropriate percentage times the actual $F_M$. This value must be used for calculating acceleration times plus fuel mileage.

If top speed is achieved in a gear at an RPM greater than maximum HP RPM, the maximum $F_D$ is used for acceleration calculations up to the maximum HP RPM. Above this RPM, $F_D$ is the appropriate percentage times the actual $F_M$. The $F_D$ maximum is used to calculate fuel mileage.

# Chapter 7: Gears and Velocity

## Cruising RPM

The engine RPM at a given velocity is dependent on the ratio of the gear being used and the effective diameter of the rear wheel.

## High-Velocity Effective Wheel Diameter

Studies made on several types of vehicles with different types of tires revealed that the increase in wheel diameter due to the centrifugal force caused by high velocity was less than 1% at 100 MPH. Thus, the measurement of wheel diameter at near-zero velocity will be adequate for performance calculations.

## Low-Velocity Effective Wheel Diameter

Wheel diameter can easily be measured using masking tape, a ballpoint pen, and a measuring tape. A motorcycle drive wheel can be measured with one person on a flat, level sidewalk. Two persons are required for a car, preferably using a deserted, flat, level parking lot.

With the vehicle in position to move one tire circumference forward, place a strip of masking tape in a vertical position at the lowest point of the tire, near the periphery. The lowest edge of the tape should be within a half-inch of the pavement. With the pen, make a vertical mark at the bottom edge of the tape. Next, place a similar piece of tape on the pavement pointing at the tape on the tire. Place a pen mark on this tape aligned with the mark on the tire. Drive or push the vehicle with a driver inside until the tire tape completes one revolution and is pointing straight down again. Place a third piece of tape pointing at the tire tape and make a pen mark aligned with the tire tape pen mark. The measured distance between the two pavement tape pen marks is the static circumference of the tire (81.33 inch on the #1 Test Vehicle). Dividing by $\pi$ (3.1416) gives a wheel diameter of 25.89 inches. Dividing by 2 gives us the effective radius of the rear wheel in inches, and dividing by 12 inches gives us the effective radius of the rear wheel in feet.

$$25.887 \text{ in} \div (2 \times 12 \text{ in/ft}) = 1.0786 \text{ feet}$$

See Chapter 13, Effective Wheel Diameter for metric radials.

## Gear Multipliers

The multiplier for the fifth gear is:

Multiplier = R primary x R final

5.6051 (overall) x 0.9394 (5$^{th}$ transmission gear) ÷ 1.0786 = 4.8817.

The multipliers for all other gears are computed in a similar fashion.

Thus, the torque calculated using methods given in Chapter 3 times the multiplier gives the gross vehicle thrust at the drive axle ($F_M$).

An alternate method of finding the multiplier when a given RPM corresponds to a given velocity is as follows:

$$\frac{N \times \pi}{V \times 44} = \frac{8426 \times 3.1416}{123.24 \times 44} = 4.8817, \text{ as previously found.}$$

## Use of Gear Multiplier

The gear multipliers convert the rotary torque forces into linear forces which are compatible with the rolling resistance, drive train loss, and aerodynamic drag.

## Wheel Spin

After calculating the gross thrust as in the previous section, subtracting the drive train loss gives the net thrust to the rear wheel. If this value exceeds the weight on the drive wheel times the coefficient of friction for the surface being used, the drive wheel may break traction and spin. This is especially true at the Salt Flats at Bonneville Speedway.

# Chapter 8: Acceleration Calculations

## Force Equation

$$F_M - F_D = F_R + F_A + F_C + F_G$$

(Refer to the symbol definitions in Appendix 4.)

## Calculating Aerodynamic Drag

Reference #1 Test Vehicle at top speed; $F_C$ and $F_G$ are zero in the force equation above at top speed.

| V | N | T | $F_M$ | $F_D$ | $F_A$ | $F_A$ @ 100 |
|---|---|---|---|---|---|---|
| 123.24 | 8426 | 40.147 | 195.988 | 19.599(.10) | 159.699 | 103.152 |

V is from data sheet for #1 Test Vehicle.

N is from data sheet for #1 Test Vehicle.

T is calculated per Chapter 3.

$F_M$ is T times the multiplier per Chapter 7 and the data sheet.

$F_D$ is 10% of $F_M$ per Chapter 4

$F_A$ is air drag in lbs at 123.24 MPH

$F_A$ @ 100 is air drag at 100 MPH per Chapter 5 as follows:

$$\frac{156.699 \times (100)^2}{(123.24)^2} = 103.152 \text{ lbs @ 100 MPH}$$

## Starting From a Complete Stop

When starting from a complete stop with a manual transmission, the following guidelines are given:

1. With a vehicle under 3,000 lbs $WT_G$ (gross vehicle weight) and a maximum speed in low gear of 33 MPH, 95% of the maximum torque should be used for acceleration until the RPM with the clutch fully engaged produces a torque higher than 95% of $T_M$.

2. With a vehicle of 2,000 to 4,000 lbs $WT_G$ and a maximum speed in low gear of 45 MPH, 90% of the maximum torque should be used as described in #1 above.

3. With any vehicle that ranges from 45 to 60 MPH in low gear, 85% of the maximum torque should be used as described in #1 above.

4. Vehicles outside the above limits should be treated on an individual basis and usually depend on limitations of the clutch.

## Acceleration Through the Gears

To determine the engine RPM in all transmission gears, proceed as follows:

1. Using #2 Test Vehicle, divide the effective wheel diameter 23.5 inches by 12 which equals 1.958333 feet.

2. Multiply by $\pi$ to get 6.1522856 feet of travel per revolution; store this in memory.

3. For convenience, use 60 MPH velocity which is 88 feet per second. Divide 88 by 6.152 in storage to get 14.303627 revolutions per second of the drive axle.

4. Multiply this times the transmission ratio (1.0) and the axle ratio (3.70) to get 52.923421. (Although this is RPS of the engine, multiplying by 60 gives engine RPM at 60 MPH. Dividing by 60 gives RPM per MPH which is the same figure.) *Caution: Some manufacturers include the top transmission ratio as part of the final drive ratios; this is true for Test Vehicle #1.*

5.  This is the RPM per MPH in 4$^{th}$ gear. Divide by the 4$^{th}$ gear transmission ratio (1.0) and multiply by 3.658, the 1$^{st}$ gear transmission ratio to get 193.59387 RPM per MPH for 1$^{st}$ gear.

6.  Multiplying this number by the velocity (in 1$^{st}$ gear) gives the 1$^{st}$ gear RPM. All other gears are handled in a similar fashion.

The shift velocities were selected as even velocities as close to the 8,500 RPM shift velocities as possible for simplicity of calculations (shift velocities; as shown on page 113, #1 Test Vehicle—Acceleration Times). The RPM for every velocity in fifth gear can be determined as follows:

$$\frac{8426 \text{ RPM}}{123.24 \text{ MPH}} = 68.370659 \text{ RPM/MPH}$$

68.370659 RPM/MPH x 110 = 7521 RPM @ 110 MPH

In first gear:

$$\frac{68.37065 \times 2.500}{0.9394} = 181.953$$

181.953 x 40 = 7278 RPM @ 40 MPH

All other gears can be calculated as above.

Two entries are made at each shift velocity to show the RPM in each gear. For simplicity, the air drag in pounds should be calculated for each velocity as follows:

$$\frac{103.152 \times (60)^2}{(100)^2} = 37.13 \text{ lbs @ 60 MPH}$$

Note that 5 MPH increments have been used everywhere except at the shift velocities. Using 1 MPH increments, the quarter-mile elapsed times were only 0.04 seconds faster and the terminal velocity only 0.05 MPH higher.

The torque can then be calculated per Chapter 3 and multiplied by the appropriate multiplier—the gear being used—to determine $F_M$. Subtracting $F_A$, $F_R$, and $F_D$, gives $F_N$: the net force for accelerating the vehicle.

Since $F_R$ and $F_D$ are constant for each gear, they may be logged in next to the gear multiplier.

When $F_N$ has been determined for the next velocity increment, the time to accelerate the 5 MPH increment may be calculated.

From general physics:

$$F = MA = \frac{W}{g} \times A$$

F = Force in lbs

$WT_G$ = Gross Vehicle Weight in lbs

Since $A = \frac{\Delta V}{t}$; $F = \frac{W \Delta V}{gt}$

$\Delta V$ = change in velocity in ft/sec

g = gravitation acceleration in ft/sec$^2$

t = acceleration time in seconds

Since W, $\Delta V$, and g are constant, $\frac{W \Delta V}{g} = 154.98$

Thus, $F_{avg} = \frac{154.98}{t}$

Acceleration Times:

The average $F_N$ between 40 and 45 MPH is found as follows:

$$\frac{479.83 + 444.64}{2} = 462.235$$

$$462.235 \div 154.98 = 2.9825461$$

$$\frac{1}{2.9825461} = 0.335 \text{ seconds}$$

All other 5 MPH acceleration times can be calculated in a similar fashion.

## Acceleration Times at Shift Velocities

$F_N$ (avg) from 45-47 MPH =

$$\frac{444.64 + 412.74}{2} = 428.69$$

$$428.69 \div 154.98 = 2.7660989$$

$$\frac{1}{2.7660989} = 0.36152 \text{ seconds for 5 MPH increment}$$

$$\frac{47 - 45}{5} = \frac{2}{5} = 0.4$$

$0.4 \times 0.36152 = 0.145$ seconds for 2 MPH

$F_N$ (avg) from 47-50 MPH =

$$\frac{309.24 + 307.30}{2} = 308.27$$

$$308.27 \div 154.98 = 1.9890954$$

$$\frac{1}{1.989054} = 0.50274 \text{ seconds for 5 MPH}$$

$$0.50274 \times \frac{3}{5} = 0.50274 \times (0.6) = 0.302 \text{ for 3 MPH}$$

All other shift velocity acceleration calculations are performed in a similar fashion.

For calculation simplicity, it is best to calculate all the $F_N$ values for RPMs below the peak torque point RPM in all gears. Next, calculate the $F_N$ value between the peak torque RPM and the maximum power RPM in all gears. Finally, calculate the $F_N$ value for RPM above the maximum power RPM. The acceleration times can then be calculated in one pass.

## Acceleration Near $V_{MAX}$

When calculating the acceleration times in 1 MPH increments just before reaching $V_{MAX}$ approximately 100% deviation in time and distance between the calculated data and the test data was revealed. The only obvious explanation of this phenomenon is that the aerodynamic drag does not behave like a mass or steady force.

The actual acceleration times near $V_{MAX}$ on several cars and motorcycles were corrected by using the final 5 MPH increment prior to $V_{MAX}$. The odd 3.24 MPH increment from 115 MPH to 118.24 MPH on #1 Test Vehicle gave the time to top speed of 38.668 seconds which closely matches the test data.

## Total Distance and Time Calculations

After the incremental times have been found and transferred to the $A_D$ pages of the #1 Test Vehicle analysis (pages 115-116), the distance and total times can be calculated. The time from 0 to 5 MPH (0.376 seconds) times the average velocity of 2.5 MPH (3.666 ft/sec given on the form) produces 1.4 feet displacement, which is also the total displacement at this point. From 5 to 10 MPH,

0.377 seconds times the average velocity of 7.5 MPH (11 ft/sec) produces 4.1 feet of displacement; adding this to the 1.4 feet of previous displacement gives a total of 5.5 feet. The procedure continues until top speed is reached.

Next, add the incremental times to get the total elapsed time. Time to speed is 38.668 seconds as mentioned before.

## Quarter Mile Elapsed Time and Terminal Velocity

These values are found by interpolation as follow:

Quarter mile = $\frac{5280 \text{ ft}}{4}$ = 1320 ft – 1144.1

(displacement at 100 MPH on page 116) = 175.9 ft ÷ 275.7

(distance traveled from 100 to 105 MPH) = 0.6380123 x 1.834

(time from 100 to 105 MPH) = 1.170 sec + 12.177

(time to 100 MPH) = 13.347 seconds elapsed time.

0.6380123 (see above) x 5 = 3.190 MPH + 100=103.190 MPH terminal velocity. This terminal velocity is achieved just as the vehicle reaches the finish line (1320 ft from start line).

All the published magazine test acceleration times are slower than calculated —yet the quarter-mile elapsed times compare. The elapsed time was 13.4 to 13.5 seconds obtained from other magazine tests and actual test data. Thus, all magazine test times are slow. Only analysis can reveal this type of deviation.

## Optimum Shift Velocities

Note how all of the $F_N$ values at the shift points do not match. Lower elapsed times and higher terminal velocities can be achieved by varying the shift velocities to more closely match the $F_N$ values. A slight over rev in the lower gear may provide a closer match. When the $F_N$ values are within 1% difference or less, the optimum shift point has been achieved. The RPM in the lower gear should not exceed the red line RPM—the maximum recommended RPM for the engine. The red line for #1 Test Vehicle is 9,300 RPM.

## Calculated Red Line RPM

If the red line RPM is not specified, the following procedure is recommended:

Reference #1 Test Vehicle

$N_L$ = 12472 RPM

$N_P$ = 8000 RPM

$\overline{\phantom{4472}}$

4472 ÷ 4 = 1118 + 8000 = 9118 RPM

If a properly tuned engine misses at this RPM or makes strange engine noises, a lower RPM should be used. Subject motorcycle was revved to 10,900 RPM (by accident) with no missing or strange noises.

## Hill Climbing

This specification is obtained by calculating $F_N$ at 65 MPH. This figure divided by the $WT_G$ gives the percent grade capabilities for the gear being used.

## Towing

Since heavy trailers often use multi-ply bias ply truck tires, the rolling resistance would be 0.029 x $WT_G$ in pounds. If radial tires are used, $F_R$ is 0.025 x $WT_G$.

Although trailers vary in size, configuration, and other factors contributing to the aerodynamic drag, estimating the drag as a proportion of the air drag of the vehicle has proven to be the easiest method of calculating trailer air drag and gives reasonably accurate performance estimates.

Given: a 3,500 lbs boat and trailer on 6-ply bias ply truck tires

$F_R$ = 0.029 x 3500 = 101.5 lbs

$F_A$ = 0.8 x 101.5 lbs = 81.2 lbs @ 60 MPH = 225.56 lbs @ 100 MPH

*(Note: The 0.8 is used because the towing vehicle causes a partial reduction in air drag—the trailer is virtually traveling in the drafting (low pressure) area of the vehicle. The 225.56 lbs of air drag should be used even if radial tires are used on the trailer.)*

Hill climbing and fuel mileage can now be calculated as shown in the previous section and Chapter 11, Power Consumption / Fuel Mileage using the new $F_R$ ($F_R$ for vehicle + $F_R$ for trailer) and the new $F_A$ ($F_A$ for vehicle + $F_A$ for trailer). The new $WT_G$ must also be used to calculate the percent grade that may be climbed.

## Summary

Since the top speed of a vehicle is often estimated or taken on a course different from the course on which the acceleration data was taken, the calculation of the air drag is often in error. If a governor was used on the vehicle, the top speed and the resultant air drag are only estimates. Since drive train loss varies from vehicle to vehicle, it is the second estimate used in calculating high-speed acceleration.

Any qualified mathematician will affirm that having two unknowns requires two equations. In the Calculating Aerodynamic Drag section in this chapter, only one equation exists for acceleration times; therefore, the two variables cannot be solved.

In defense of the "two equations, two unknowns" concept, the acceleration times at high speed truly define the acceleration characteristics of the vehicle. Furthermore, the drive train loss is linear, or constant, throughout the velocity range per Chapter 6. Since the air drag varies as the square of the velocity per Chapter 5, a few empirical (trial and error) calculations can be made to match the drive train loss and the air drag with the acceleration times.

# Chapter 9:
# Automatic Transmissions

## Preliminary Research

Since automatic transmissions were first produced in the late 1930s, very little data has been published on how they operate. Motors manual explained the sequence of shifting the planetary gears and clutches of a hydra-matic transmission to obtain the four forward speeds. No data was given regarding the fluid coupling. No data was given on torque converters except for the torque converter ratio, which was inadequately defined.

## Early Measurements—Fluid Coupling

A tachometer connected to an engine idling in drive revealed that the fluid coupling allowed the 400 RPM idle to increase to 800 RPM at full throttle. At approximately 11 MPH, 1600 RPM, the engine RPM appeared to match the RPM of the transmission input shaft. Although no multiplication was produced, the increased RPM allowed higher engine torque to drive the transmission.

## Torque Converter Measurements

On the Torque Converter data sheet of #3 Test Vehicle is an analysis of the torque converter. Using an electric tachometer and a calibrated speedometer, the RPM versus velocity data were taken. Although the data were somewhat erratic, a general pattern was detected. A graph (shown on page 123) was made with RPM (in hundreds) as the vertical component, and velocity in MPH was the horizontal component. A circle with the center on the zero velocity line was drawn through the 1,200 RPM point and continued until it joined the RPM versus velocity line for the low gear. The trigonometric derivation is shown on page 123 in the Appendices and the example calculations can be used for any three-element torque converter.

The 2.1 torque converter ratio was taken from a local library publication and verified by a magazine publication. The 2.1 multiplier ratio compared approximately with the RPM ratio. Thus, 1200 RPM ÷ 2.1 = 571 RPM was not exactly the measured idle RPM but could be used for calculation purposes.

Although the low gear drive train loss was 25%—typical for the planetary gears—another 10% loss was used on the torque converter. Thus, the 2.1 ratio became 1.8900. The difference in RPM as calculated on page 123 for 5 MPH became:

$$1227 - 382 = 845$$

$$\frac{845}{1200} = 0.7041667 \times (1.890 - 1) = 0.6267 + 1 = 1.6267$$

multiplier. All multipliers and revised drive train losses are done in a similar fashion.

If a torque converter ratio cannot be found, assume a value and calculate the 0-30 MPH and 40 MPH acceleration times. Adjust the ratio to match the test times.

# Chapter 10:
# Internal Engine/Accessory Friction

## Preliminary Research

According to the textbook *Applied Thermodynamics* by V.M. Faires[1], the friction HP of a test engine was made by driving the engine with the dynamometer. Adding this power to the power output gives the indicated HP.

This assumption appears incorrect due to the following data from the text:

|  | At 1200 RPM | At 3600 RPM |
|---|---|---|
| Output power | 33 | 80 |
| Friction power | 6 | 35.5 |
| Indicated power | 39 | 115.5 |
| Indicated torque | 170.69 (calculated) | 168.50 (calculated) |

A 1.28% drop in torque over a 2,400 RPM range using any technology available today is **not** feasible. The net fuel consumption figures also indicate that the friction horsepower is **not** feasible.

---

1  Faires, V. M., Applied Thermodynamics. The McMillan Company, New York, 1962, page 130.

## Dynamometer Measurements

The dynamometer data given for #1 Test Vehicle included fuel consumption data throughout the RPM range. This data combined with various low and high speed fuel consumption tests on #2 Test Vehicle gave a good starting point for subject studies.

## Internal Engine/ Accessory Friction Formula

A total of seven engines were used to generate a formula for internal friction. Fuel consumption tests were made at the highest feasible velocity in addition to tests made at or near the peak torque RPM. Basic torque data was taken by cranking the dead engine over, with spark plugs removed, using a calibrated torque wrench at approximately 10 to 15 RPM, then estimating the torque at 1,000 RPM from the slopes of the torque versus RPM curves for all seven engines. From this data the 12 or so number of variables was reduced to three— B, S, and number of cylinders.

After approximately 50 sets of variables were tried, the following formula evolved:

Torque at 1000 RPM = $\dfrac{BSN}{2.85}$ = 14.970 lb-ft for #2 Test Vehicle.

Additional torque at maximum power RPM = $\dfrac{BSN (N_p - 10)}{200}$ = 9.173 lb-ft

for #2 Test Vehicle. Total engine friction torque = 24.143 lb-ft at 5300 RPM.

The effects of this friction on fuel consumption are given in Chapter 11. The seven engines ranged from 27 to 900 HP in order to cover a large range of friction.

# Chapter 11:
# Volumetric Efficiency/Fuel Consumption

## Preliminary Research

In a normally aspirated (non-supercharged) piston engine, the maximum torque is approximately proportional to the volumetric efficiency—see Appendix 4: Symbol Definitions for more detail. The quantity of air/fuel mix is also dependent on the volumetric efficiency. The only published information on this subject is on custom dynamometer tests, which included a flow meter to measure the incoming air flow.

## Early Measurements

Measurements made on #2 Test Vehicle only provided an estimate of air/fuel mix temperature of 109° F, just as the intake valve closed with an ambient temperature of 68° F and $P_B$ = 29.98 in-Hg. Measurements taken at 3,600 RPM on the fuel consumed at maximum throttle and 13.1 lbs-air/lbs-fuel gave estimates of 94.996 $in^3$ of air fuel mix in two revolutions of the engine. This calculates to 83.728% volumetric efficiency (Hot) and 76.655% at $T_A$ = 60° and $P_B$ = 29.92.

Fuel consumption then becomes 0.003 $E_V$ DfN where f is the fuel factor.

At 16.0 lbs-air/lbs-fuel, $f = \dfrac{1}{2.31} = 0.4329$—liquid cooled engines.

At 13.6 lbs-air/lbs-fuel, $f = \dfrac{1}{\dfrac{13.6 \times 2.31}{16.0}} = 0.50929$—air cooled engines.

$E_v$ at the hot temperature was used to keep the 0.003 constant an even number. The volumetric efficiency remains quite constant from the peak torque RPM down to about 1800 RPM. Tests were not made below this RPM due to the severe vibration caused by the 4-cylinder engine.

## $E_V$ Calculations

The calculations proceed as follows:

Refer to #2 Test Vehicle

$$E_V = \frac{T_M \times \sqrt{8.5} \times 0.85}{\sqrt{R_C} \times \text{Disp.}} = \frac{115 \times 2.9154759 \times 0.85}{3.0 \times 113.45779} = 0.83728 \text{ (Hot)}$$

For engines with a one-cylinder displacement over 35.0 in$^3$, the calculations proceed as follows: (Reference #3 Test Vehicle)

$$E_V = \frac{T_M \times \sqrt{9.0} \times 0.85}{\sqrt{R_C} \times \text{Disp.}} = \frac{245 \times 3 \times 0.85}{3.0413813 \times 283.03786} = 0.7257564 \text{ (Hot)}$$

## Fuel Consumption Above Maximum Torque RPM

The volumetric efficiency above the peak torque RPM became complicated by the increase in internal engine friction and the decrease in overall volumetric efficiency—see Chapter 10. The fuel consumption for the #2 Test Vehicle at the maximum torque RPM is calculated as follows:

$C_f = 0.003\ E_V\ \text{DFN} = 0.003 \times 0.83728 \times 113.45779 \times 0.4556847 \times 36.0 = 4.6751253$ gal/hour

Using $BSN_C$ of 42.6636, calculate the internal friction (Chapter 10) for 67.023 MPH (3,600 RPM) as follows:

$$\frac{BSN}{2.85} + \frac{BSN (36-10)}{200} = 14.9697 + 5.5463 = 20.516 \text{ lb-ft}$$

Add the torque output:

115.0 + 20.5160 = 135.516 lb-ft

$$\text{Power} = \frac{135.516 \times 36}{52.52} = 92.889838 \text{ HP}$$

## Gross Specific Fuel Consumption

Since the gross fuel consumption divided by HP/hours is approximately constant above the maximum torque RPM, it is calculated as follows:

$$\text{SFC gross} = \frac{C_F @ 3600}{P_T @ 3600} = \frac{4.6751253}{92.88938} = 0.05033 \frac{\text{gallon/fuel}}{\text{HP/hour}}$$

Fuel consumption at 70 MPH which is 3705 RPM.
Calculate the torque at 3705 RPM per Chapter 3.

$$\frac{(37.05-36)^2 [(115-106.031)]}{(53-36)^2} - 115 = 114.966 \text{ lb-ft}$$

$$\text{Internal friction} = \frac{42.6636}{2.85} + \frac{42.6634 (37.05-10)}{200} = 20.740 \text{ lb-ft}$$

$$\text{Power (total)} = (114.966 + 20.740) \times \frac{37.05}{52.52} = 95.733 \text{ HP}$$

x SFC gross = .05033 = 4.8182 gal/hour at 70 MPH

## Power Consumption / Fuel Mileage

The total of $F_A$ (105.71), $F_R$ (77.72), and $F_D$ (80.132), the values with 370 lbs of passengers and luggage gives a total force of 263.562 lbs. Dividing by the $F_M$ for 70.

$$\frac{263.562}{434.42} = 0.6067 = \text{Efficiency x } C_F \text{ Max} = 4.8182 = 2.9232 \text{ gal/hour}$$

$$\text{MPG} = \frac{70 \text{ MPH}}{2.9232 \text{ gal/hour}} = 23.95 \text{ MPG}$$

Fuel mileage for higher velocities is done in a similar fashion.

When the efficiency exceeds 0.70, both carbureted and fuel-injected engines have richer mixtures. On #2 Test Vehicle, the mixture ranged from $\frac{15.2 \text{ lbs-air}}{\text{lbs-fuel}}$ at 0.70 efficiency to 13.1 at 0.95 efficiency.

$$\text{At 85 MPH, E} = 0.7380 - 0.7 = \frac{0.0380 \text{ x } 2.1 \text{ (15.2 to 13.1)}}{0.25 \text{ (0.95 to 0.70)}} = 0.3192 - 15.2$$

$$= 14.881 \frac{\text{lbs-air}}{\text{lbs-fuel}} \quad \frac{15.2}{14.881} = 1.0214 \text{ times normal } C_F$$

Thus, the calculations are made in the normal fashion, then corrected as above for the richer mixture.

Most throttle body injected or carbureted engines used a 15.2 mixture—slightly leaner than the 15.05 stoichiometric (ideal) air fuel mixture. Most multi-port fuel injected and large (over 20 cubic inches per cylinder) engines use 16.0 mixtures for maximum efficiency.

# Chapter 12:  Gross Horsepower and Torque Correction—Prior To 1973

## Preliminary Research

Prior to 1973, most U.S. manufacturers gave gross HP and torque specifications on the engines used in their vehicles. The conditions used to achieve these specifications were not given or referenced, and conditions probably varied between manufacturers.

In an unknown publication in the mid 1950s, a photograph of an alleged factory dynamometer room was shown. From the photo, the following was observed:

### Systems

- **Intake system**—no air cleaner used. Engine was isolated from radiator, etc. to provide cool intake air.
- **Exhaust system**—exhaust manifold, pipes and mufflers were not used. A steel plate header with four straight pipes was bolted onto each side of the V8 engine. The pipes went straight out from the exhaust ports for about 10 inches, then curved and pointed up and to the rear, very similar to those used on 1990s AA fuel dragsters. The pipes pointed high near the ceiling where the exhaust gases were removed with fans.

### *Accessories*

- **No belts were used**—the remote coolant pump was driven by an electric motor plugged into the wall socket. A plate was mounted on the engine in place of the coolant pump to prevent leakage.
- The remote electric generator was driven by an electric motor plugged into a wall socket. The remote battery was charged in conjunction with a remote voltage regulator.
- The remote electric fuel pump was operated off of the battery. A plate was mounted on the engine where the mechanically driven fuel pump went to prevent oil leakage.
- The ignition was powered by the remote battery.

## Gross HP and Torque Variation

From the above description of the test conditions, it is apparent that the gross specifications are considerably higher than the specifications that would exist after the engine is installed in the car with the correct intake, exhaust, and accessory systems.

The manufacturer's justification for this test procedure was low cost. A thorough examination of the procedure should reveal that very little labor was saved using it compared with the actual systems. Using the actual systems for testing gives the net or crankshaft HP of the engine, which has been used from 1973 on.

## Gross to Net HP Conversion

On all 1960 through 1973 vehicles studied, the net HP was 7/8 or 0.875 times the gross HP. #3 Test Vehicle was rated at 195 HP @ 4,800 RPM.
0.875 x 195 = 170.625 HP. This figure was rounded to 170.

The HP RPM is directly proportional to the square root of the torque at maximum power.

Torque at 4800 = 195 x $\dfrac{52.52}{48.00}$ = 213.3625 lb-ft.

$\sqrt{213.3625}$ x X = 4800  maximum HP RPM

RPM constant X = 328.61107

At 170 HP, torque = 170 x $\dfrac{52.52}{45.86}$ = 194.73064 lb-ft.

$\sqrt{194.73064}$ x 328.61107 = 4586 RPM, this is rounded to 4600 RPM.

## Gross to Net Torque Conversions

On all 1960 through 1973 vehicles studied, the net torque was 6/7 or 0.8571429 times the gross torque. #3 Test Vehicle was rated at 285 lb-ft at 2800 RPM. 0.8571429 (6/7) x 285 = 244.286 lb-ft. This is rounded to 245 lb-ft.

The torque RPM is directly proportional to the torque. Previous studies of the 283 in$^3$. Chevy engine revealed that 285 lb-ft of torque occurs at 3,400 RPM. Thus, $\dfrac{3400}{285}$ x 245 = 2923 RPM. This is rounded to 2,900 RPM.

## Other Gross to Net Conversions

An analysis of a 1956 Oldsmobile with a 324 in$^3$ V8 and a 4 BBL carburetor revealed the following:

The 240 gross HP was **not** 210 net using the 0.875 factor. The actual net HP was 205 @ 4200 RPM. (-2.38%)

The 350 lb-ft gross torque was **not** 300 net using the 0.8571 factor. The actual net torque was 290 @ 2400 RPM. (-3.33%)

From *Marks' Standard Handbook for Mechanical Engineers, 11th Edition* (Mc-Graw-Hill, 2006) the graphic net values of the 1950 Oldsmobile—303.7 in$^3$ V8 with a 2 BBL carburetor revealed the following:

HP: gross 135; net 120 (0.8889) (+1.59%)

Torque: gross 263; net 240 (0.9125) (+6.46%)

Analysis of this vehicle proved the values to be correct. Thus, the vehicles of the 1950s should not be taken as predictable as the 1960s and up. Torque and HP must be proven from actual test data as was done above.

Foreign manufactured vehicles did **not** conform to the above specifications. Empirical (trial and error) studies were made to determine the torque and HP of #2 Test Vehicle.

# Chapter 13: Shortcut Procedures for Performance Specifications

## Published Performance Specifications

The acceleration times, top speed, quarter-mile elapsed time and terminal velocity are reported in tests published in various car magazines. If the potential buyer is willing to accept the fuel mileage and hill climbing capability, no calculations are needed.

## Approximate Fuel Mileage and Hill Climbing Specifications

If these are the only specs desired, proceed as follows: (Reference #1 Test Vehicle)

- Solve for the air drag per Chapter 9, Early Measurements—Fluid Coupling Section.
- Verify the air drag by using the value obtained above and calculate high speed acceleration to verify the value. The highest speed acceleration for #1 Test Vehicle is from 90 to 100 as shown on page 113 of the test sheet. 12.9 − 9.8 = 3.1 seconds. Calculated value is 2.811 seconds. 70 to 80 = 7.7 − 6.5 = 1.2 seconds. Calculated value is 1.580 seconds. Since one value is low and the other is high, they are assumed to cancel each other out, and the air drag is assumed to be correct.
- Calculate $F_N$ per Chapter 8 to obtain 114.862 lbs at 65 MPH using $F_A$ sitting up, which is approximately 22.5 lbs higher at 100 MPH than when

the rider is crouched down on the fuel tank for high speed runs. Divide by $WT_G$ of 680 lbs to obtain 16.891% grade climbing capability which is 1.00% higher than the actual value since the $F_D$ for sitting up is higher than the 20.831 lbs when crouched.

- Calculate volumetric efficiency (Hot) per Chapter 11, $E_V$ Calculations. Calculate maximum fuel consumed at 65 MPH, 4444 RPM using the formula: $0.003\ E_V\ DfN$.

  $f_n = 0.50929$ for a 13.6 air/fuel mixture

  $0.003 \times 0.81057 \times 44.9423 \times 44.44 = 2.4735$ gal/hour

  $92.407\ (F_N) \div 208.696\ (F_M) = (E)\ 0.44278 \times 2.4735 = 1.0952$ gal/hour

  $\dfrac{65\ \text{MPH}}{1.0952} = 59.34$ MPG which is 1.54% higher than actual value, since the $F_D$ for sitting up is higher than the 20.831 lbs, when crouched.

## Acceleration at Low Speed In a Tall Gear

Reference #1 Test Vehicle traveling at 30 MPH (2911 RPM) in 3rd gear. Proceed as follows:

- Calculate torque at 2,911 RPM per Chapter 3, Torque Below the Maximum Torque RPM section to obtain 38.829 lb-ft.
- Calculate $F_N$ which is 210.457 lbs ÷ 680 = 0.3095 "G." This value can be compared with other vehicles.

## Recommended Cruising Velocities

Whether cruising on a flat road or climbing a hill in a lower gear, the steady velocity should **not** exceed 90% of maximum HP at full throttle for that RPM. In top gear on a flat road, 85% of maximum HP is preferred. Calculate per Chapter 3, Torque Between the Maximum Torque RPM and the Maximum Power RPM section.

## Passing Capabilities

In the mid 1970s, each new vehicle had passing capabilities published and delivered with the vehicle. The data included the distance traveled to pass a 75-foot long truck traveling 50 MPH on a two-lane road without exceeding 80 MPH. The time in seconds to perform this task was also given.

With new interstate freeways constantly being upgraded to four lanes or better, this practice of testing and publishing passing capabilities was discontinued. For drivers who spent most of their driving time on two-lane roads, this data was gone. The time and distance given was from a point 100 feet behind the truck (1.36 seconds at 50 MPH), a truck length of 75 feet, and 150 feet in front of the truck before moving out of the passing lane. Using #2 Test Vehicle, second gear is inadequate since it is so close to shift point, a new $F_N$ is calculated for 50 MPH in 3$^{rd}$ gear:

3713 RPM

T= 114.960 lb-ft

$F_N$ = 353.44 lbs 50 to 55 MPH

t = 1.65 second (+ 0.096)

d = 127.4 feet (+ 7.4)

The following data can then be calculated:

a.   50 MPH x 1.4666 $\dfrac{(88 \text{ ft/sec})}{(60 \text{ MPH})}$ = 73.33 ft/sec

b.   80 MPH x 1.4666 = 117.33 ft/sec

c.   Car acceleration time (50 to 80 MPH) = (21.024 − 7.955) + 0.096 = 13.165 seconds

d.   Car acceleration distance (1620.9 − 333.3) + 7.4 = 1295.0 ft

e.   Truck travel time = 13.165 seconds (see section c above)

f.   Truck travel distance = 13.165 x 73.33 (see section a above) = 965.4 ft

g.   Car minus truck distance = 1295.0 (see section d above) − 965.4 = 329.6 ft

h.  Car distance to pass truck = 325.0 ft (100 + 75 + 150)

i.  Car minus truck distance = 329.6 (see section g above) – 325 = 4.6 ft

j.  Car minus truck time = 4.6 ft ÷ 117.33 (see section b above) = 0.039 seconds

k.  Total passing time = 13.165 seconds (see section c above) – 0.039 = 13.126 seconds

l.  Total passing distance = 1295.0 (see section d above) – 4.6 ft (see section i above) = 1290.4 ft

Thus, #2 Test Vehicle took 13.126 seconds and 1290.4 feet in the passing lane to clear the truck. This task was performed with a lone driver; no data was given for a full load of passengers plus luggage. This figure would vary considerably depending on the size of the car and engine.

If a driver is concerned about passing capabilities fully loaded, a new 50-80 MPH acceleration run can be calculated and the new distances can be found. Since the distance in most cases will exceed a quarter mile (1320 feet), the driver's judgment becomes very critical.

## Fuel Mileage With a Lone Driver

Using #2 Test Vehicle, substitute $F_D$ and $F_R$ for the lone driver, and then add $F_A$ of 105.71 lbs at 70 MPH to give a new $F_t$ of 258.632 lbs. Dividing by 434.421 lbs ($F_M$) gives a new E of 0.5953 x 4.8182 = 2.8685 gal/hour.

$$\frac{70}{2.8685} = 24.40 \text{ MPG}$$

## Effective Wheel Diameter

Instead of the procedure given in Chapter 7, Low-Velocity Effective Wheel Diameter section, the approximate diameter of a metric radial can be found as follows:

Given: Metric radial P195/70-R14.

Proceed as follows:

[195 x 0.03937] x 0.7 = 5.3740 in tire height x 2 + 14 (wheel diameter) x 0.97 (average deflection) = 24.006 inches.

# Chapter 14:
# Summary—Beware of Pitfalls

The procedures described herein often appear too complex and sometimes redundant due to the published data. After over 40 years of studying published data, it appeared that more incorrect test data and performance specs existed than correct test data and performance specs. Examples are as follows:

### Top Speed

Chapter 9, Early Measurements—Fluid Coupling section, shows how critical the air drag is on top speed. One or two miles per hour can cause a large deviation in $F_A$. A *Car & Driver* test of a 1994 Saleen Mustang showed a top speed of 147 MPH. The acceleration data given on the same test indicated a top speed of approximately 157.3 MPH. This condition is not *Car & Driver*'s fault: due to the high speeds and long distances required, the acceleration data is taken on one track, and the top speed on another.

A similar condition exists with cars that have a governor to limit top speed. This is usually done to avoid exceeding the velocity ratings of the tires used. Thus, a higher $F_A$ must be assumed and verified with acceleration data.

## Acceleration Times

#1 Test Vehicle proved that all published times were incorrect! Using the magazine test times produced a quarter-mile elapsed time of about 14.0 seconds. Usually only one or two times are off, generally at high speeds where air turbulence throws the times off.

## Displacement Times

These quarter-mile elapsed time and terminal velocity figures have been proven to be the most accurate of any performance data. They were not in general use prior to 1970.

## Horsepower

Ford gave the horsepower specs of the 1994 Mustang GT as 215 HP @ 4,200 RPM. Analysis using *Car & Driver*'s road test revealed 215 HP @5,000 RPM.

## Torque

Ford gave the maximum torque spec of the 1986 Taurus V6 engine as 160 lb-ft. Analysis using *Car & Driver*'s road test revealed 170 lb-ft.

## Fuel Mileage

These estimates are discussed in Chapter 11, $E_V$ Calculations section.

## Drive Train Loss—$F_D$

Note the large corrections on #2 Test Vehicle for gears 1, 2, and 3. The gear loss would cause trouble if it were being used to verify $F_A$. Analysis of the *Car & Driver* road test of the 1994 Nissan Sentra revealed $F_{D2}$ as 17%, $F_{D3}$ as 15%, and $F_{D4}$ as 15%. Analysis was very difficult since the governed top speed of 110 MPH was achieved in both 4th and 5th gears.

## Transmission Ratios

These are often not available—even in the library. If performance is desired on the owner's car, a calibrated electric tachometer can be used to accurately estimate the transmission ratios by matching RPMs with calibrated velocities in all forward gears.

## Gear Ratios, Tire Size, and RPM

A *Car & Driver* test report on an 1982 Volkswagen Scirocco showed shift RPMs of 6,700 in three gears. The given HP was 74 at 5,000 RPM. Chapter 3, Torque Above the Maximum Power RPM section shows a normal "No load" RPM of 7,210 RPM which would give normal redline of 5,550 RPM. This is far short of the 6,700 RPM where the shift was reported as being made. Extending the HP RPM 16.5% gives a HP RPM of 5,825 RPM. The $N_L$ for this RPM is 8,604 RPM. This figures extends the redline to 5,900 RPM, still short of the 6,700. The high speed (80-90 MPH) acceleration using the 6,700 RPM shift RPM gave in excess of 20 seconds compared with the 10.2 seconds of the test results. By changing the shift velocities and RPMs to approximately 5,900 RPM, the test results were achieved.

## The "Normal" Performance Analysis

When a magazine test report on a vehicle is used for a performance analysis, seldom is it ever completed in one set of calculations. Of the nearly 150 documented vehicle analyses completed, an average in excess of four sets of calculations were made in order to closely match the test data. Many of the deviations have been noted in this chapter. Only a few of the vehicles had minor deviations from the test data. Even though #1 Test Vehicle had normal calculations in almost every area (1 HP deviation), the calculated acceleration times were all different from the magazine test times. Thus, the 400-plus analyses made proved the "normal" in order to provide a computer program that can give rapid results. Deviations from normal can be treated as discussed in this and previous chapters.

# Chapter 15: Reciprocating Weight

## Preliminary Research

During RPM studies of engines of the 1950s and the 1960s, it appeared that most car engines followed a general pattern. The long stroke engines achieved the maximum HP at a lower RPM than a similar shorter stroke engine. The engines with larger cylinder bores achieved the maximum HP at slightly lower RPM than a similar smaller bore engine.

One of the exceptions was the British Jaguar DOHC in-line 6 cylinder. The maximum HP of 176 was rated at 4,750 RPM with a 3.626-inch bore and a 4.173-inch stroke. Compared with other engines, the maximum power should have been achieved at about 3,500 RPM, not 4,750. The only possible explanation was that the reciprocating weight of this engine was extremely low. It was apparent that the ratios and proportions being used would not work when the reciprocating weight was not "Normal."

## Power Discrepancies

From 1973 on, the auto manufacturers gave net power and torque ratings—the output with the engine driving all of its normal accessories plus a standard inlet and exhaust system. Theoretically, these numbers could be used with regular analysis procedures to determine vehicle performance. In general, this was true. However, several manufacturers gave conservative figures, which produced large errors in the calculated performance. Obviously, a formula for calculating engine RPM was needed which included variations in reciprocating weight.

### "Normal" Reciprocating Weight

A library manual was found that gave guidelines to all the necessary dimensions of an automotive piston. An auto magazine was found that gave connecting rod weights. This was not useful since the majority of the weight was the hollow cylindrical shape that supported the rod bearing. The rod-bearing support is considered rotating weight; only the shank of the rod extending from the bearing support is reciprocating weight. Finally, an isometric scale drawing of an engine was found that had views of all the internals plus cutaway views showing the internal parts of the piston. Using a copy machine with enlarging capabilities, the views were "blown up" several times to enable accurate dimensions to be obtained. From these dimensions and material densities, the volumes and weights of the reciprocating parts were determined. Next, a complete stress analysis was made on all affected sections of the piston, wrist pin, con rod shank/beam, and the con rod bearing. Next, the entire cycle was repeated using a smaller bore. All dimensions were scaled down, then stress analyzed to maintain stresses similar to the original engine. Final results: the weights of the two sets of parts calculated were approximately proportional to the square of the bore. Now, if a longer stroke was used, the shank/beam of the con rod would be longer, which would increase the weight. This deviation was quickly dismissed since a 10% increase in con rod shank/beam length only increases the reciprocating weight 1.24%.

### Weight Proportions

To verify the calculations, sets of reciprocating parts of a known engine were obtained from a junk yard. The bearing support on the con rod was removed on a band saw. The joining surfaces were ground smooth. All parts weighed 751.6 grams (1.6570 lbs).

Thus, the bore $(3.307 \text{ inches})^2$ x $0.1515145 = 1.6570$ lbs. This is the "normal" $W_R$ formula.

Piston = 48.34%

Rings = 7.18%

Wrist pins & keepers = 13.55%

Con rod shank/beam = 30.93%

# Chapter 16:
# Horsepower RPM Formula

## Preliminary Research

The early studies of RPM where the maximum HP and torque were achieved began with comparisons of other engines. This system of ratios and proportions gave good results when the reciprocating weights were "Normal" as discussed in Chapter 15. If a correction factor for reciprocating weight were added, it would not explain why the maximum HP peaked at a specific RPM. The original assumption that the volumetric efficiency reached a peak, then dropped rapidly, did not seem logical since many engines turned over 35% higher RPM than the maximum power RPM.

## Natural Frequency System

The simple spring mounted solid on one end with a weight fastened on the other end is a typical oscillating system described in various physics and engineering mechanics books.

The formula is given as follows:

$$f_n = \frac{1}{2\pi} \frac{\sqrt{kg}}{w}$$

$f_n$ = natural frequency of the system in cycles/sec

k = spring rate (a force exerted divided by the resultant deflection) in lbs/in

g = gravitational acceleration = 386 in/sec$^2$

w = weight in pounds

Thus, if a spring requires 1.0 lbs to deflect it 4.0 inches, the rate is k = ¼ = 0.25 lbs/in. If a 0.5 lb weight is fastened on one end the frequency will be:

$$f_n = \frac{1}{2\pi} \frac{\sqrt{(0.25 \times 386)}}{0.5}$$

$f_n$ = 2.21 cycles/sec

This same principle can be applied to the piston engine. The K for the crankshaft can be found by using the reciprocating weight for the engine discussed in Chapter 2 combined with the "g" force at the maximum power RPM. The reciprocating weight for the engine with a 3.307-inch bore was 1.657 lbs.

## "G" Forces of Crankshaft

The engine described in the Natural Frequency System section of this chapter had a stroke of 3.228 inches and developed maximum power at 4,800 RPM. The "g" forces are found as follows:

4800 RPM ÷ 60 = 80 RPS

1/80 = 0.0125 sec per revolution

Distance/rev = 3.228 x π = 10.141 inches

10.141 inches ÷ 0.0125 = 811.285 in/sec

Average acceleration in ¼ rev = $\dfrac{811.285}{\dfrac{(0.0125)}{4}}$ = 259,611.2 in/sec$^2$

Peak acceleration = π x 259611.2 in/sec$^2$ ÷ 386 = 1056.47 G

Maximum force = 1056.47 x 1.657 = 1750.57 lbs

1750.57 lbs ÷ S/2 = 1750.57 lbs ÷ 3.228 = 1750.57 = 1084.61 lbs/in

## "K" Required for Engine

Substituting the known values in the frequency formula given in the Natural Frequency System section of this chapter:

$$f_n = \frac{1}{2\pi} \sqrt{(1084.61 \times 386 \div 1.657)} = 80 \text{ cycle/sec}$$

80 cycle/sec x 60 sec/min = 4800 RPM

This formula explains why the power is frequency—or RPM—sensitive. At RPMs below 4,800, the engine torque and resultant force on the piston divided by the fixed stroke must be higher than 1084.61 lbs/in. The K for the piston then decreases with RPM due to the reduction in volumetric efficiency and the increase in internal engine friction. At 4,800 RPM the piston is pushing the crankshaft with the same K for the crankshaft. Above 4,800 RPM, the K for the piston continues to decrease while the crankshaft K is increasing. Thus, the piston is trying to push the crankshaft that is now trying to move faster than the piston. This explains why the power rapidly falls off after this natural frequency is reached.

## Mean Effective Pressure Studies

The K for the piston at 4,800 RPM was considerably more difficult to determine than anything previously discussed in this chapter. The only feasible way to determine the K for the piston is to make mean effective pressure studies. These studies were made using "Charles Law[1]":

$$\frac{P_1 V_1}{T_1} = \frac{P_2 V_2}{T_2}$$

where P = absolute pressure (gauge + atmospheric) in PSI

V = Cylinder volume above piston in inches$^3$

T = absolute temperature (actual + 459.7°) in °F

1  Faires, V. M., *Applied Thermodynamics*. The McMillan Company, New York, 1962.

The crankshaft rotation was studied every 9° of rotation to give 20 data points in 180°. Figure 2 below gives the piston stroke, the angle between the center line of the con rod and cylinder, and the lever arm length on the crankshaft for each 9° of rotation.

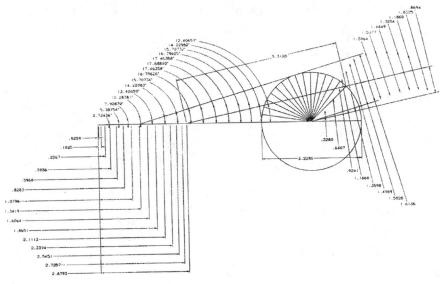

Figure 2

$V_1$ in the equation of "Charles Law" is the clearance volume of the cylinder:

3.6968 in³. $V_2$ is the piston area: $\dfrac{\pi(3.307)^2}{4} = 8.5893$ in².

This value multiplied by the stroke for 9°, which is 0.0259 inch, yields 0.2225 in³. Add 3.6968 in³ (clearance volume) to get 3.9193 in³. The absolute temperature was assumed to be linear—the same drop for each 9° of rotation. By assuming $P_1$, $P_2$ could be found from the above data. At each 9° of rotation, the pressure multiplied by the piston area gave the total force on the piston. Multiplying this force by the cosine of the pressure angle (2.72436° for 9° of rotation) gives the force on the connecting rod. Multiplying the connecting rod force by the crankshaft lever arm (0.3280 inch for 9° rotation) gives the torque at 9° crankshaft rotation. This procedure is repeated for the remaining 14 data points. Since the exhaust valve opens around 45° before bottom center, (135° after start of rotation) no further data is needed. The $P_1$ is then adjusted to provide an average torque of 87.533 lb-ft averaged over the data for 180° of rotation. The 87.533 lb-ft @ 4,800 RPM equals the 80 HP produced by the engine. Adding the first 9 piston forces and dividing by ten gives the average piston force for the first 90° of rotation. The first piston force is not

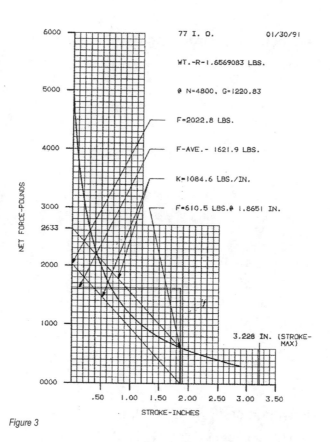

Figure 3

used since it takes at least 9° for the pressure to build up. By adjusting both $P_1$ and the temperature drop, the K of 1084.6 lbs/in for the piston can be found as shown in Figure 3 above. The piston stroke for 90° is 1.8651 inches, caused by the side effects of the connecting rod. The average force of 1621.9 lbs minus 610.5 lbs (at 90° rotation) is 1011.4 lbs. Add this to the 1621.9 lbs average to get a peak of 2633.3 lbs. 2633.3 – 610.5 lbs = 2022.8 lbs, which when divided by the stroke of 1.8651 inches = 1084.6 lbs/in, the K that matches the K for the crankshaft.

This entire study was made on another engine with a larger bore. Although the peak pressures are proportional to the square of the bore (assuming the same volumetric efficiency), the K for the second engine proved to be directly proportional to the bore.

## Variation of Reciprocating Weight with Stroke

An increase in stroke causes force changes with the same reciprocating weight. The calculations of the "G" Forces of Crankshaft section are repeated with a 10% increase in stroke, i.e., 3.5508 inches.

4800 RPM ÷ 60 = 80 RPS

1/80 = 0.0125 sec per revolution

Distance/rev = 3.5508 inches x $\pi$ = 11.1552 inches

11.1552 inches ÷ 0.0125 = 892.413 in/sec

Average acceleration in ¼ rev = 892.413 = 285,572.3 in/sec$^2$

Peak acc. = $\pi$ x 285,572.3 = 448,575.9 in/sec$^2$

448,575.9 in/sec$^2$ ÷ 386 = 1162.11 G

Max force = 1162.11 x 1.657 lbs =1925.62 lbs

(3.5508) x 1750.57 (page 64) = 1925.6 lbs

Thus, the effective reciprocating force is proportional to the length of stroke.

## Derivation of HP RPM Formula

From the studies made in this and the previous section, the following data are determined:

- The K for the engine caused by the piston is directly proportional to the bore.
- The K for the engine is inversely proportional to the stroke.
- The K for the engine is proportional to the torque per cubic inch.
- The effective reciprocating weight is directly proportional to the stroke.

Inserting these data into the formula gives:

$$f_n = \frac{1}{2\pi} \sqrt{\frac{B}{3.307}} \times T_P \div [\pi B^2 S N_C \times 1084.6133 \times 386]$$

$$\frac{[S \div 3.228] \times [87.533 \div 110.90517]}{W_R \dfrac{(S)}{3.228}}$$

Multiplying the above formula by 60 to give cycles (revolutions) per minute gives the following:

$$N_P = K_P \sqrt{(T_P \div BS^3 N_C W_R)}$$

$N_P$ = RPM where maximum HP is achieved

$T_P$ = Torque at maximum HP RPM– lb-ft

$B$ = Bore in inches

$S$ = Stroke in inches

$N_C$ = Number of cylinders

$W_R$ = Reciprocating weight (one cylinder) in pounds

$K_P$ = Power constant = 13930.0

This formula has been used on over 300 engines. Although there are minor variations when using an aluminum head versus cast iron, the deviations appear to be negligible. The formula works on all 4-cycle engines, L-Head, overhead valve, overhead cam, any number of cylinders, any type of fuel (diesel, methanol, gasoline, Nitro methane, etc.), and normally aspirated or supercharged (roots blower or single and/or dual turbochargers).

Variations in altitude causes loss of power, but the formula still works because $T_P$ is included in the formula.

This formula has been used to verify power and RPM estimates when dynamometer data were not available. Conversely, several manufacturers' power and RPM specs have been proven incorrect; correct data was determined by performance analysis.

## HP RPM Formula

For #1 Test Vehicle engine use the following formula:

$$8000 = 13{,}930 \sqrt{([42.6725] \div [2.401 \times (2.480)^3 \times 4 \times W_R])}$$

To obtain $W_R$, store 42.6725 ($T_p$) in calculator memory, divide 8,000 by 13,930 to obtain 0.5743, and square it to get 0.32982. This removes the square root sign on the right side of the equation. Multiply 0.32982 x 2.401 x (2.480)$^3$ x 4 = 48.315328.

Divide by the 42.6725 (in memory), and take the reciprocal (1/x) to give $W_R$ = 0.8832083 lbs/cylinder. Using $T_p$ = 1, the formula for $N_p$ = 1224.6612 $\sqrt{T_p}$,

# Chapter 17:  Torque RPM Formula

## Preliminary Research

The early studies of torque RPM revealed that the ratios and proportions used for HP RPM did not work. In addition, the torque RPM is achieved between a low RPM (2,500 or less) and an RPM approaching the HP RPM for some motorcycle engines (7,000 RPM for maximum torque, 8,000 RPM for maximum HP). The proportion used for many engines produced torque RPMs higher than the HP RPM on small motorcycle and several formula one engines. Thus, it was known up-front that the torque RPM would be difficult to calculate.

## "G" Forces of Crankshaft

The engine referenced in Chapter 16, Derivation of HP RPM Formula section, had a stroke of 3.228 inches and developed maximum torque (95 lb-ft) at 3,000 RPM. The "g" forces are found as follows:

3000 RPM ÷ 60 = 50 RPS

1/50 = 0.02 seconds per revolution

distance/revolution = 3.228 x $\pi$ = 10.141 inches

10.141 inches ÷ .02 = 507.053 in/sec

Average acceleration in a ¼ revolution = $\dfrac{507.053}{\dfrac{(0.20)}{4}}$ = 101,410.6 in/sec$^2$

Peak acceleration = $\pi$ x 101410.6 = 159295.4 in/sec$^2$

159,295.4 in/sec$^2$ ÷ 386 = 412.68 G

Maximum force = 412.68 x 1.657 = 683.81 lbs

683.81 lbs ÷ S/2 = 683.81 lbs ÷ (3.228 ÷ 2) = $\dfrac{683.81}{1.614}$ = 423.67 lbs/in

## "K" Required for Engine

Substituting the known values in the frequency formula given in Chapter 16, "G" Forces of Crankshaft.

$$f_n = \frac{1}{2\pi} \sqrt{(423.67 \text{ x } 386 \div 1.657)} = 50 \text{ cyc/sec}$$

50 cyc/sec x 60 = 3000 RPM

Since this RPM is in the mid-range of the engine, there was no apparent reason for the maximum torque to be achieved at this RPM. The only assumption that could be made was that the volumetric efficiency was at the maximum. Above 3000 RPM, the volumetric efficiency would decline while internal engine friction was on the increase.

## Mean Effective Pressure Studies

The subject studies were made as described in Chapter 16, Derivation of HP RPM Formula section. The $P_1$ is adjusted to provide an average torque of 95.0 lb-ft averaged over the data for 180° of rotation. Plotting the piston forces (pressure times area) for the entire power stroke produces a graph as shown in Figure 4. By adjusting both $P_1$ and the temperature drop, the K of 423.65 lbs/in (rounded from 423.67) can be achieved at a piston stroke of 1.8651 inches which occurs at 90° after start of rotation. Note that the slope line is tangent to the force curve at mid-stroke.

This entire study was made on another engine with a larger bore. Since the two graphs appeared very similar, a considerable amount of trial and error was used to derive a working formula.

## Derivation of Torque RPM Formula

From the studies made in the two previous sections plus the ratios and proportions used during the preliminary research, the following data were determined:

a. The K for the engine caused by the piston is less than 0.5% and is dropped by the Formula.

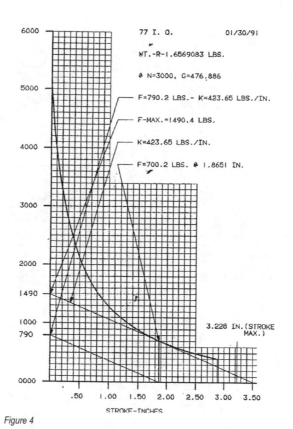

*Figure 4*

b. The K for the engine is inversely proportional to the square of the stroke.

c. The K for the engine is proportional to the square of the torque per cubic inch.

d. The effective reciprocating weight is directly proportional to the stroke. See Chapter 15, "Normal" Reciprocating Weight section.

Item (c) above indicates that the torque RPM is directly proportional to the maximum torque. This feature is in opposition to everything learned about torque RPM up to this time. Although it appears controversial, the following derivation with the appropriate correction factors will show that all 4-cycle engines are covered using the derived procedures.

Inserting the above data into the formula gives:

$$f_n = \frac{1}{2\pi} \sqrt{\dfrac{\left[\dfrac{T_M}{\dfrac{\pi B^2 S N_C}{4}}\right]^2 \times 423.67 \times 386}{\dfrac{(S)^2 \times [95.0 \div 110.90517]^2}{(3.228)^2}} }$$

$$\dfrac{W_R (S)}{3.228}$$

Multiplying the above formula by 60 to give cycles (revolutions) per minute gives the following:

$$N_T = K_T \sqrt{\dfrac{(T_M)^2}{B^4 \, S^5 \, N_C^2 \, W_R}}$$

$N_T$ = RPM where maximum torque is achieved

$T_M$ = maximum torque in lb-ft

B = bore in inches

S = stroke in inches

$N_C$ = number of cylinders

$W_R$ = reciprocating weight (one cylinder) in pounds

$K_T$ = torque constant (33290.0)

This formula has been used on over 250 engines with excellent accuracy. Subject engines had torque RPM ranges from 2,000 to 7,000 RPM.

Using $W_R$ = 0.8832083 lbs/cylinder found in Chapter 15, Weight Proportions, and using 1 for $T_M$, the torque RPM for #1 Test Vehicle becomes:

$$N_T = 33290 \sqrt{\dfrac{(1)^2}{(2.401)^4 \times (2.480)^5 \times (4)^2 \times 0.8832083}}$$

$N_T = 158.60202 \, T_M$

## Deviations from Torque RPM Formula

### High Torque—Long Stroke Engines

500cc Triumph and BSA motorcycle engines produce torque according to the formula up to torque values equal to 0.9 times the displacement in cubic inches. This condition leads to the following correction:

When the stroke to bore ratio is 1.20 to 1.30, use a base torque of 0.9 x displacement = 0.9 x 30.432 = 27.389 lb-ft

With an actual torque of 39.4 lb-ft, subtract 27.389 to get 12.011, divide by 3 to produce 4.004 and add 27.389 to end up with 31.393 lb-ft. Multiply this value by the regular torque formula for the correct value.

When the stroke to bore ratio is 1.10 to 1.20 (650cc Triumphs and BSAs), use the above procedure but divide the excess torque by 2.

Although these procedures appear rather crude, these high performance engines have very flat torque curves—usually within 1.5% of the peak torque (normal dynamometer deviation) for about 1,200 RPM. Thus, a calculation error of 100 RPM would not affect the performance analysis of the vehicle.

### "L" head (Flat-head) Engines

A study of the 1950s flat-head engines revealed that the torque RPM calculations on most were too high. Actual manufacturers' specs should be used on these engines. The Ford V8 torque RPM did work with the formula.

### Calculate Torque RPM from 7,000 to 9,000 RPM

Subtract the 7,000 RPM from the value calculated. Multiply the difference by 0.484, then add the calculated value to 7,000 RPM to obtain the correct torque RPM.

Example:  Harley Davidson (1992) X R750:

$N_T$ calculated = 7360

7360 – 7000 = 360

360 x 0.484 = 174

174 + 7000= 7174 (round to 7150 RPM: maximum torque RPM)

### Calculated Torque RPM from 9000 RPM and over

Divide the calculated torque, measured in hundreds, by 200. Take the square root and multiply by 0.0019. This gives the RPM loss formula. Multiply this by the calculated RPM (in hundreds) squared. This gives the RPM loss. Subtract from calculated $N_T$ calculated to give actual $N_T$.

Example: Kawasaki (1996) ZX-11:

$N_T$ calculated = 10100 RPM

$\sqrt{(101 \div 200)}$ x 0.0019 = 0.0013502

0.0013502 x $(101.00)^2$ = 13.77

101.00 – 13.77 = 8723 RPM (round to 8700 RPM: maximum torque RPM)

The above deviation formulas are based on a minimum of three engines with known specifications. It is unknown at this time if the formula deviations hold true for extreme RPMs such as the Jaguar V-10, which develops 860 SAE HP @ 17,500 RPM. When specs become available, corrections may be made.

### Torque RPM for Turbocharged Engines

All torque RPM deviations are based on the 1978 Cosworth DFX. Dynamometer data was published in *Machine Design* magazine, which was only distributed to industries. Tests were conducted with the same engine with varying boost pressures. These three sets of data, plus others, give the correction given as follows:

| Vehicle | Displacement | Disp. Corr. | $N_T$ (Calc) | $N_T$ Corr | Nmax (calc) | N/loss (max) |
|---------|--------------|-------------|--------------|------------|-------------|--------------|
| 78 DFX | 161.26928 | 1.0 | 27.808045 | ___ | 198.44 | 99.22 |
| 82 DFX | 161.26928 | 1.0 | 35.13971 | | 223.07 | 111.54 |

Calculations for the 1982 Cosworth DFX are as follows:

$$\frac{N_T\ (82)}{N_T\ (78)} = \frac{35.13971}{27.808045} = 1.2636527$$

$$\sqrt{(1.2636527)} \times 198.44 = 223.07\ N_T\ \text{max}$$

$$\sqrt{(1.2636527)} \times 99.22 = 111.54\ N_L\ \text{max}$$

$$N_T\ (\text{calc}) = 354.0\ (\text{max torque}) \times 35.13971 = 12439$$

$$(124.39 \div 223.07)^2 = 0.3100486$$

$$0.3100486 \times 111.54 = 34.68\ \text{RPM N/loss}$$

$$124.39 - 34.68 = 89.71\ \text{RPM} = N_T\ (\text{round to 8950 RPM: maximum torque RPM})$$

This figure matched the spec given in *Machine Design* magazine.

Since the torque RPM formula varies with the number of cylinders, a correction is needed when the number of cylinders is not 8. The data for the 1978 DFX and the 1973 Drake Offy (both 4-cylinder) are given as follows:

| Vehicle | Displacement | Disp. Corr. | $N_T$ (Calc) | $N_T$ Corr | Nmax x $\sqrt{0.70711}$ | N/loss (max) |
|---------|--------------|-------------|--------------|------------|------------------------|--------------|
| 4 cyl 78 DFX | 80.63464 | 1.0 | 55.616091 (2x) | — | 166.87 | 84.43 |
| 73 Offy | 159.44466 | 1.9773718 | 35.9787 (2x) | 71.143265 | 188.73 | 94.32 |

$$\frac{\text{Displacement (73 Offy)}}{\text{Displacement (78 4 cyl DFX)}} = \frac{159.44466}{80.63464} = 1.9773718$$

$$1.9773718 \times 35.9787 = 71.143265$$

$$71.143265 \div 55.616091 = 1.2791849$$

$$\sqrt{1.2791849} \times 166.87 = 188.73 \; N_T \; \text{Maximum}$$

$$\sqrt{1.2791849} \times 84.43 = 94.32 \; N \; \text{Loss Maximum}$$

$$73 \; \text{Offy} \; N_T \; (\text{calc}) = 510.0 \; (\text{max torque}) \times 17.98935 = 91.75 \; (\text{in hundreds})$$

$$(91.75 \div 188.73)^2 = 0.2363362$$

$$0.2363362 \times 94.32 = 22.29 \; N \; \text{Loss}$$

$$91.75 - 22.29 = 69.46 \; (\text{round to 6900 RPM: max torque RPM})$$

This is the torque RPM given by *Machine Design* magazine.

In summary, each turbocharged engine has its own torque formula. As the torque is increased with increased boost pressure, the RPM is also increased. However, the loss of RPM varies as the square of the RPM, which makes each engine have its own torque-versus-RPM curve. By using the 78 DFX as a base, the displacement and number of cylinder variations are used to correct the effective value of $N_T$. This was not necessary for the 82 DFX. The ratio of $N_T$

(82 DFX) to $N_T$ (78 DFX) is 1.2636527. The square root of this times 198.44 gives 223.07, the N maximum for the 82 DFX. Thus, if the $N_T$ calculated for the 78 DFX were 19,844 RPM, the actual RPM would be 19,844 – 9,922 = 9,922 RPM. The values for the 82 DFX are 22,307 – 11,154 = 11,153 RPM. The values for the 73 Offy are 18,873 – 9437 = 9436 RPM. When a lower value of $N_T$ is used, follow the calculations previously described.

### Torque RPM for Engines with Roots Blowers

These calculations are made using the procedures given in the section above.

# Chapter 18:
# Calculation Discrepancies

## Introduction

With a strong automotive background plus all the formulas and procedures given in this publication, it would appear that an acceleration analysis using a published test report could be made in about an hour using just a pocket calculator, or about 20 minutes using a CD-Rom program in a computer. After nearly 200 vehicle analyses were completed, not one was found without correction for various discrepancies. The closest to "normal" was the 85 Ford Mustang GT; only one correction was made to match the test data, and that was the revving of the engine above the maximum HP RPM.

During the early studies of vehicle performance, a standard form titled "Calculation Discrepancies" was made to keep track of various changes in the data. Each form had summaries of data for five different analyses. Some of the toughest analyses had as many as four discrepancy sheets. The number of sheets was considerably reduced after the torque and HP RPM formulas were developed.

## Horsepower and Torque RPM Deviations

In 1979, General Motors released the Chevy Citation as a 1980 Model (along with the Pontiac Phoenix, Oldsmobile Omega, and Buick Skylark—the "X" cars) and the new V6 with the following specs:

Bore = 89 mm = 3.504 inches

Stroke = 76 mm = 2.992 inches

Displacement = 2836.84 cc = 173.113 inches$^3$

Power = 115 HP @ 4800 RPM

Torque = 145 lb-ft @ 2400 RPM

### Using the HP RPM formula:

$$4800 = K_P \sqrt{\frac{125.829}{3.504(2.992)^3\,(6)W_R}}$$

$$\frac{(4800)^2}{(13930)^2} = 0.1187354 = \frac{125.829}{563.119W_R}$$

$W_R$ = 1.8819164 (1.0116212 x the "normal" reciprocating weight)

$N_P = 427.90816\ \sqrt{T_P}$

### Using the Torque RPM formula:

$$N_T = K_T \sqrt{\frac{(T_M)^2}{(3.504)^4\,(2.992)^5\,(6)^2W_R}}$$

$N_T = 21.273057\ T_M$ = 3085 RPM (round to 3100 RPM)

Using the torque formula (for values < $N_T$) we find the torque at 2400 RPM.

$$\frac{145\,(24.00\,)}{52.52} - \left[\frac{(31.00-24.00)^2\ \text{x}\ 145\ \text{x}\ 5}{52.52\,(31-5)^2}\right] = 65.260\ \text{HP} = 142.810\ \text{lb-ft}$$

This torque is 98.49% of the maximum, which is technically correct. It should be noted here that 1979 was a very important year for "fuel mileage" and low-RPM torque with smaller engines and taller gears were the "in" thing.

In 1985, the Chevy V6 of the same dimensions had the following specs:

Power = 130 HP @ 4800 RPM

Torque = 160 lb-ft @ 3600 RPM

Using the formula $N_P = 427.90816 \sqrt{T_P}$ developed earlier, the 130 HP would be achieved at 5000 RPM. Analysis of the 85 Pontiac with the V6 engine proved this RPM to be correct.

Using the formula $N_T = 21.273057\, T_M$, the torque RPM is found to be 3404 RPM (rounded to 3400 RPM).

Using the torque RPM formula (for values > $N_T$) we find the torque at 3,600 RPM

$$T = 160 - \frac{23.448}{(50-34)^2}\,(36-34)^2 = 159.634 \text{ lb-ft}$$

This torque is 99.77% of maximum, which is technically correct.

Note here that the difference in torque RPM of the two similar engines was 3400 − 3100 = 300 RPM; yet GM specified the torque RPM difference at 3600 − 2400 = 1200 RPM.

The most confusing of all the specs was the 1987 engine, which was reduced in power by 5 HP. The torque spec remained the same. The new power rating was given at 125 HP @ 4500 RPM.

Using the formula $N_P = 427.90816 \sqrt{T_P}$, the correct RPM should be 4935 RPM (round this to 4950 RPM). Analysis of an 87 Pontiac 6000 with the V6 engine revealed that 4950 RPM was the correct figure.

The specs on the 85 Ford Mustang GT V8 were as follows:

Bore = 4.000 inches

Stroke = 3.000 inches

Displacement = 301.593 inches$^3$

Power = 210 HP @ 4600 RPM

Torque = 265 lb-ft @ 3400 RPM

Solving for $W_R$ gives 2.5448314 lbs (1.0497474).

Solving for $N_T$ gives 10.458543 $T_M$ = 2772 RPM (2800 RPM rounded).

Using the torque formula T @ 3400 RPM produces 262.196 lb-ft. This torque is 98.94% of maximum which is technically correct.

The 94 Ford Mustang V8 of the same dimensions had the following specs:

Power = 215 HP @ 4200 RPM

Torque = 285 lb-ft @ 3400 RPM

The power is up 5 HP from 1985, yet RPM is down 400 RPM?

$N_P$ for the 1985 is 297.07406 $\sqrt{T_{P'}}$ If the same is used for 1994, $N_P$ = 4635 RPM.

$N_T$ = 2980 RPM

Using these calculated RPMs in an acceleration analysis, the calculated times were slower than the test times published by *Car & Driver* magazine in a test report. To match the test times, the same HP was used but the RPM was increased to 5000 RPM. This gave a $W_R$ of 2.0288113 lbs. The torque RPM with this revised $W_R$ gave $N_T$ = 3300 RPM.

The $W_R$ using the 94 spec was 3.4229755 lbs (1.41198 x the "normal" reciprocating weight.). The $N_T$ for this $W_R$ is 2570 RPM (rounded to 2600 RPM).

These specs would indicate that the reciprocating weight was increased over 40% to handle 5 more HP and 20 lb-ft more torque.

## Procedure Recommended

Due to these types of discrepancies, the engine specs should be checked before starting an analysis procedure. Although the torque RPM deviation has negligible effect with the manual transmission, the actual calculated torque specs give more accurate low-end torque when an automatic transmission is used.

# Chapter 19:  Torque Drop

## Introduction

During studies made on high RPM fuel consumption, another study, "Internal Engine/ Accessory Friction," was made to enable calculation of fuel consumption. To avoid calculation of volumetric efficiency at high RPM, the term "Gross Specific Fuel Consumption" was introduced. Using $SFC_G$, the fuel consumption at any RPM up to the maximum power RPM could be found. The volumetric efficiency can also be determined using $SFC_G$.

## Torque Drop Definition

During the studies of various high RPM engines, it was found that the reduction in volumetric efficiency from the maximum torque RPM to the maximum power RPM was considerably less than a standard passenger car engine. This condition was especially true for engines with 4 valves per cylinder. Also, the reduction in *gross* torque from the maximum torque RPM to the maximum power RPM was proportional to the change in volumetric efficiency. This reduction in gross torque within the RPM limits given will hereafter be called the "Torque Drop."

## Application of Torque Drop

Further studies of torque drop found that the drop was directly proportional to the maximum torque. This seems logical since the volumetric efficiency and maximum torque are proportional to each other. It was also found that the drop was proportional to the square of the power RPM. This also seems logical since the volumetric efficiency was reduced in proportion to the square of the RPM. The final finding, and the most difficult to comprehend, was that the drop is proportional to the square of the RPM difference between the maximum torque RPM and the maximum HP RPM. Furthermore, all of these conditions hold true only when the factors that affect engine breathing are held constant. This means that the same fuel induction system, same inlet port size, same valve size (and number of valves), and same exhaust system are used. Most important of all, the same cam and valve train must be used. If any of these factors are changed, the torque drop will be changed.

These rules or guidelines were established on the 1978 Cosworth V8 Indianapolis engine. The same engine was used with three different boost pressures.

a.  85 MM mercury absolute (26.97 psi gauge) was used for maximum performance with minimum engine degradation. This would apply to qualifying and passing during the race.

b.  80 MM mercury absolute (24.52 psi gauge) was used for passing in traffic and overtaking slower cars.

c.  70 MM mercury absolute (19.62 psi gauge) was used for normal racing. The engine provided 1.8 MPG at this power which was needed to finish the 500-mile race with the maximum of 280 gallons of methanol allowed for each car.

With torque and HP data for each of the above boost pressures, the torque drop was clearly defined. Further studies revealed that the guidelines were also applicable to normally aspirated engines.

Although the torque drop study was originally made to determine torque and horsepower with varied boost pressure, the study provided the following:

1.  Power variation with altitude.

2.  Power variation with various fuels.

3.  Power variation with displacement and compression ratio changes.

Thus, the rather insignificant and difficult study of torque drop opened up a field of engine analysis that could previously only be estimated. The dynamometer data taken on numerous motorcycle engines years earlier appeared very logical and normal when the torque drop figures were applied.

# Chapter 20:
# High Altitude Compensation

## Introduction

From *Marks' Standard Handbook for Mechanical Engineers*[1] the following data were obtained:

| Altitude in feet | Atmospheric Pressure in inches/Hg |
|---|---|
| Sea Level | 29.92 (1.000) |
| 1000 | 28.91 |
| 2000 | 27.91 |
| 3000 | 26.90 |
| 4000 | 25.90 |
| 5000 | 24.89 (0.832) |
| 6000 | 24.03 |
| 7000 | 23.17 |
| 8000 | 22.30 |
| 9000 | 21.44 |
| 10,000 | 20.58 (0.6877) |

---

1   *Edited by: Avallone, E.A.; Baumeister, T., III Marks' Standard Handbook for Mechanical Engineers (10th Edition). Mc-Graw-Hill, 1996.*

From the same handbook, the following formula was obtained:

$$P = \frac{1.3263 \, P_B}{(T_A + 459.70°)}$$

P = air density (lbs/ft³)

$P_B$ = Barometer pressure (in-Hg)

$T_A$ = Ambient Temperature (°F)

459.70 = constant to convert temperature to absolute temperature °F

Using the density formula, the standard density at sea level is:

$$P = \frac{1.3263 \times 29.92}{(59 + 459.70°)}$$

P = 0.0765045 lbs/ft³

$$\frac{P_B}{\rho} = \frac{29.92}{0.0765} = 391.088 \text{ (pressure to density ratio)}$$

At Bonneville Salt Flats in September, $P_B$ = 26.40 (4200 ft) and $T_A$ = 95 °F

$$P = \frac{1.3263 \times 26.40}{(95 + 459.70)} = 0.063123 \text{ lbs/ft}^3$$

$$\frac{P_B}{\rho} = \frac{26.40}{0.063123} = 418.231 \text{ (+6.94%)}$$

## Effects on Volumetric Efficiency

During the upper half of the intake stroke, the air/fuel mix had a 6.94% advantage in pressure over the sea level conditions:

Thus, $E_V$ (upper half) = $1.0694 \times \dfrac{0.063123}{0.076505} = 0.8824$ of sea level P

The $N_p$ ratio is $\dfrac{9550}{10500} = 0.90952$

$0.90952^2 = 0.82723$

Since the RPM and resultant piston velocity is reduced (see the following section), the kinetic energy of the air/fuel mix is reduced proportional to the square of the velocity.

Thus, $E_V$ (lower half) = $1.0694 \times 0.8824 \times 0.82723 = 0.7806$
$E_V$ upper = $0.8824$
$E_V$ lower = $0.7806$
$0.8824 + 0.7806 = 1.6630$
$1.6630 \div 2 = 0.8315$, which is 0.77% higher than the density ratio.

The above figures indicate that the increased pressure to the density ratio of the air/fuel mix is cancelled by the reduced kinetic energy caused by the reduced RPM at maximum power, both at 4,200 ft altitude. The result is that the volumetric efficiency and resultant torque are directly proportional to the air density.

## Example of Altitude Compensation

The Kawasaki ZX-11 engine provided the following specs at sea level:

$P_B$ = 29.92 in Hg

$T_A$ = 59 °F

$\rho$ = 0.0765045 lb/ft³

B = 2.992 in (76 mm)

S = 2.283 in (58 mm)

Displacement 62.406 in³ (1052.46 cc)

| $T_D$ | $\Delta N$ | $N$ | $T_L$ | $T_N$ | $T_T$ | $N_c$ | $P$ |
|---|---|---|---|---|---|---|---|
| | | 87.00 | 20.106 | 81.000 | 101.106 | 87.23 | |
| 0.0185574 | 18.0 | 105.00 | 27.565 | 72.528 | 95.093 | 105.00 | 145.00 |

$W_R$ = 0.8963709

$N\rho$ = 1232.9276

$N_T$ = 124.68723

At 4,200 ft:

T = 95°F

$\rho$ = 0.063123

K = 0.83007

$T_D$ = 0.0127424

| $N_c$ = 83.83 | $\Delta N$ | $N$ | $T_L$ | $T_N$ | $T_T$ | $N_c$ | $P$ |
|---|---|---|---|---|---|---|---|
| $N_L$ = 7.14 | | 76.50 | 18.672 | 67.236 | 85.908 | 76.69 | |
| $N_T$ = 76.69 | 19.0 | 95.50 | 21.267 | 60.040 | 81.308 | 95.53 | 109.174 |

24.71% of the 145 sea-level horsepower was lost by raising the altitude to 4,200 ft and the temperature to 95°F.

# Chapter 21:
# Effects of Fuel on Torque and Horsepower

## Introduction

Several years back in an unknown magazine was an article that stated "Converting an engine to alcohol fuel will increase the power about one-third." Ten years later it still was a mystery on how the article arrived at those conclusions. In 1964 Ford announced the new DOHC V8 for the Indianapolis 500. An article published in *Machine Design* magazine read, "A 40% mix of nitro methane and methanol increases the horsepower approximately 25%." It went on further to read, "After about 3 ½ minutes at maximum track speed (using the 40% nitro mix), the engine burned a hole in the piston." A performance analysis of this car revealed that the percentage of full throttle acceleration was less than 50%. This, theoretically, meant that only 1.75 minutes (105 seconds of full throttle) burned out the engine. These and other published "facts" will be addressed as the various fuels are presented.

## Methanol Fuel (Methyl Alcohol)

The use of methanol fuel in an engine requires a higher compression ratio than that needed for gasoline. A 12.5-14.5 to 1 ratio is ideal depending on altitude;

a lower ratio (11.5-13.5 to 1) is preferred if a higher percentage (over 40%) of the nitro methane is to be used. This increased compression ratio normally represents the largest power increase. For instance, if the ratio is raised from 9.5:1 up to 12.0:1, the torque will increase about 12.4%. Thus, the torque is directly proportional to the square root of the compression ratio. The methanol by itself only accounts for about 8% of the increase. The two combined provide about a 21.4% increase in torque. Since the power RPM is proportional to the square root of the torque at maximum power, this increases the total power to about 33.7%, which closely matches the data from the article mentioned in the introduction. However, the torque drop was not included. Using the Kawasaki ZX-11 at 4,200 ft and 95°F as shown in Chapter 20, Example of Altitude Compensation section we have:

| $T_D$ | $\Delta N$ | $N$ | $T_L$ | $T_N$ | $T_T$ | $N_C$ | $P$ |
|---|---|---|---|---|---|---|---|
| | | 76.50 | 18.672 | 67.236 | 85.908 | 76.69 | |
| 0.0127424 | 19.0 | 95.50 | 21.267 | 60.040 | 81.308 | 95.53 | 109.174 |

Since the compression ratio is 11.0:1, only the 1.08 methanol correction is used:

| $T_D$ | $\Delta N$ | $N$ | $T_L$ | $T_N$ | $T_T$ | $N_C$ | $P$ |
|---|---|---|---|---|---|---|---|
| | | 80.00 | 19.150 | 72.615 | 91.765 | 80.06 | |
| 0.014789 | 19.0 | 99.0 | 21.746 | 64.680 | 86.426 | 99.16 | 121.922 |

The above indicates an 11.67% increase in power. This is relatively low since there was no change in compression ratio. The increased torque only increased the maximum power torque RPM by 3.66%.

The fuel consumption has a large increase when using methanol. The fuel factor in the fuel consumption formula for a maximum power mix is 1.0908 for methanol compared with 0.5287 for gasoline—a 106.32% increase in fuel consumption.

## Ethanol Fuel (Ethyl Alcohol)

The use of ethyl alcohol, like methanol, requires a 12.0:1 compression ratio. Unlike methanol, there is no appreciable increase in torque. If the 109.17 horsepower engine in the previous section were converted to ethanol, the power would decrease by about 3% since the compression ratio is only 11.0:1. The principal advantage of ethanol is the increased fuel mileage. The fuel factor for a maximum power mix is 0.8331, which is about 76.4% of the factor for methanol but still about 57.6% higher than gasoline.

Ethanol can be distilled from corn and many other natural materials. Methanol is a petroleum derivative, despite the misleading name "wood alcohol". When gasoline production decreases, the nation may run its cars on ethanol.

## Nitro Methane / Methanol Mixes

The fuel consumption of nitro methane is about the same as methanol. At 1997 prices of $30.00 per gallon, it is not for economical purposes. For 1964, Ford recommended a 12.5% mix of nitro methane to methanol, which increased the power of the Indy 500 engine from 525 horsepower on plain methanol to 565 horsepower on the 1/8 nitro mix—1 part nitro to 7 parts methanol. Ford had run this mix on their dynamometer simulating the Indy 500 track configuration. After 500 miles with no pit stops and no yellow caution flags, the dismantled engine showed no major degradation.

This 12.5% mix had raised the torque 5.0%. This combined with the 2.4% increase in the maximum power RPM produced the 565 horsepower. Since the power is approximately proportional to the percentage of nitro, the Ford engine was reexamined using 40% nitro. The resultant horsepower was 660 HP which is 25.7% higher than the 525 HP produced on straight methanol. This calculation confirmed the Ford article and set up the formula for calculating both torque and horsepower using any mix of nitro-methane/methanol.

The torque increase is calculated as follows:

% nitro x $\dfrac{0.16}{0.40}$ + 1

For example, at 40%, 0.4 x $\dfrac{0.16}{0.40}$ + 1 = 1.16 x $T_M$ (standard).

Using the Kawasaki ZX-11 at 4,200 ft and 95° using methanol as previously shown in the Methanol Fuel (Methyl Alcohol) section of this chapter, a 40% nitro mix is added to produce the following:

| $T_D$ | $\Delta N$ | $N$ | $T_L$ | $T_N$ | $T_T$ | $N_C$ | $P$ |
|---|---|---|---|---|---|---|---|
|  |  | 89.5 | 20.448 | 84.233 | 104.681 | 89.84 |  |
| 0.0200424 | 17.5 | 107.00 | 22.839 | 75.705 | 98.543 | 107.27 | 154.235 |

At this point, the engine has been returned with slightly higher power than it had at sea level. Since the air density is reduced by the density ratio, the aerodynamic drag is 82.5% of the sea level drag. With proper gearing and a corrected fuel induction system, the revised top speed would be approximately 191.5 MPH (176 sea level stock). That is the good news. The bad news is that after 7 runs with complete cooling between each run, the engine would be subject to burning a piston or valve.

## Torque RPM with Engines of 4 or Less Cylinders

When 40% or more nitro-methane is used with methanol, the torque RPM is reduced due to the excessive heat and the lack of power stroke overlap. The 4-cylinder DFX is used as a base for these modifications:

| Vehicle | Displacement | Displacement Correction | $N_T$ Calculation | $N_T$ Correction | N Max x $\sqrt{0.70711}$ | N Loss |
|---|---|---|---|---|---|---|
| 4 cyl 78 DFX | 80.63464 | 1.0 | 55.616091 | ___ | 140.32 | 70.16 |
| 52 % Nitro 98 ZX-11 Kawasaki | 64.2065 | 0.7962645 | 102.97299 | 81.993735 | 170.38 | 85.19 |

To obtain the N Max and N Loss for the 98 Kawasaki ZX-11 racing engine using 52% nitro, divide the displacement by 80.63464 (DFX 4 cyl) to obtain 0.7962645. Multiply this by 102.97299 ($N_T$) to obtain 81.993735. Divide by 55.616091 (DFX 4 cyl) to obtain 1.4742808. Multiply the square root of this value by 140.32 to obtain N Max of 170.38 and N Loss of 85.19.

With a crankshaft torque of 117.3 lb-ft, the $N_T$ (Calc)—117.3 x 102.97299 = 120.79 RPM. Divide by 170.38 to obtain 0.7089447. Square this value and multiply it by 85.19 to give the N Loss of 42.82. $N_T$ = 120.79 – 42.82 = 77.97 RPM. Round to 7800 RPM. This compares with the dynamometer data for this engine. If the calculated torque is below 9000 RPM, use the math given in Chapter 17, Deviations from Torque RPM Formula. (Calculate Torque RPM from 7000 to 9000 RPM.)

# Chapter 22: Turbocharger Effects on Torque and Horsepower

## Introduction

After many manufactures downsized their cars and engines in the late 1970s and early 1980s, the emphasis was on fuel economy. After the "gas crunch" appeared to have stabilized, greater emphasis was put on increased power. Since many cars designed for 4-cylinder engines could not accommodate a V6 or in-line 6, turbo charging became the answer to more power.

Many people today are under the impression that the manufacturers merely added the turbo charger and associated "plumbing" to the engine. In reality, the entire engine was modified considerably. Typical changes included a modified crankshaft and all new internals—piston, wristpins, and connecting rods. Some engines required a revised valve train to accommodate the increased RPM of the turbo charged engine. All engines were designed for use with higher-octane fuel to prevent detonation caused by the increased combustion pressures. In addition, the compression ratio was reduced from about 9.5:1 to about 8.1:1 for the same reason. This single feature meant that the turbo engine would not achieve the fuel mileage of the normally aspirated engine. Conversely, the typical normally aspirated V6 would not achieve the fuel mileage or the maximum power of the turbo 4-cylinder. This is why the manufacturers claimed the best of both worlds: the turbo 4 had more power and higher fuel mileage than the optional V6.

## Turbocharged Gasoline Engines

A typical turbo 4-cylinder was the Chrysler 2.2 liter Shelby engine. The specs were as follows:

|  | Turbo | Normally Aspirated |
|---|---|---|
| **Power** | 174 HP @ 5200 RPM | 93 HP @ 4800 RPM |
| **Torque** | 200 lb-ft @ 3000-4000 RPM | 122 lb-ft @ 3200 RPM |

The specification not given was that the reciprocating weight of the turbo engine was 47.2% higher than that of the normally aspirated engine. This was needed to keep stresses on the internals down due to the 63.9% increase in torque.

In 1992, Chrysler added dual balance shafts to reduce harmonic vibration of the engine and increase the power to 224 HP @ 6000 RPM.

## Turbocharged Methanol-Fueled Engines

This type of engine is normally used only for racing. Probably the most successful of this type of engine is the 1978 Ford Cosworth DFX engine. It produced the most wins at the Indianapolis 500 of any V8 at that time. A modified version of this engine was the 1988 Illmor-Chevrolet, which produced six wins at the Indianapolis 500. Since specs were not available on this or later engines, the specs for the 1978 Cosworth DFX are given as follows:

Bore = 3.373 inches

Stroke = 2.256 inches

Displacement = 161.269 in$^3$

Boost pressure = 80 in-Hg absolute (24.52—psi gauge)

(This pressure was limited by a "pop-off" valve used during qualifying only, and not used during the race.)

Power = 850 HP @ 9800 RPM

Torque = 479 lb-ft @ 8800 RPM

A study of the turbo engine and a comparable normally aspirated engine revealed that the torque output was about the same when the turbo engine was at 20 in-Hg boost pressure.

Using the 161.26928 $in^3$, the same torque in lb-ft would be produced at $R_C$ = 8.5, $E_V$ = 85.0% (Hot), and with gasoline fuel. Converting to base torque, $R_C$ for this engine is 7.50.

$$161.269 \times \sqrt{7.5} \div \sqrt{8.5} \times \frac{0.880}{0.850} \times 1.08 \text{ (methanol)} = 169.379 \text{ lb-ft}$$

Note: the 0.88 volumetric efficiency is 0.05 less than the 0.93 (hot) volumetric efficiency estimated. This correction is required for determining the base torque for all turbocharged engines. The maximum torque was found to be the ratio of the boost pressure raised to the 0.75 power.

$(80 / 20)^{0.75}$ = 2.8284

2.8284 x 169.379 = 479.08 lb-ft = the spec for 80 in-Hg boost.

The torque RPM calculated is 13,322 RPM. Using the $N_T$ (Max) of 19,844, $(133.22 \div 198.44)^2$ = 0.4507

Using the $N_L$ (Max) of 99.22,

99.22 x 0.4507 = 44.72 torque RPM loss.

133.22 ($N_C$) – 44.72 ($N_L$) = $N_T$ = 8850 RPM (round to 8800 RPM)

At 80 in-Hg boost, the Cosworth was rated at 850 HP at 9,800 RPM. This figure was used to calculate $W_R$ = 2.9604 lbs, which is 1.7174 times the "normal" reciprocating weight. This $W_R$ was used to calculate the torque RPM formula. The torque drop of this engine was 0.20502 and was used to determine the HP RPM of the Cosworth at 85 and 70 in-Hg boost.

The same base torque of 169.38 lb-ft at 20 in-Hg was used for the 85 and 70 in-Hg boost pressure. The ratio of the boost pressures, maximum boost divided by 20 inches of Hg raised to the 0.75 power was used to find the maximum torque. The torque RPM was found as shown on page 103. The HP RPM was found using the torque drop found above for the 80 in-Hg boost. Finally, the $T_p$ times the RPM ÷ 52.52 gives the final HP.

Since no "pop-off" valve was used during the race, boost pressure was unrestricted. The Cosworth could take 85 inches of boost "safely", which produced 900 HP @ 10,000 RPM. However, the 280 gallon maximum limitation per car forced the Cosworth to use 70 in-Hg boost to get the 1.8 MPG needed to finish the race.

The 4-cylinder Drake-Offy could take 105 in-Hg boost "safely," which produced 1,024 HP @ 9200 RPM. This feature made the Offy the power "King" at the Indy 500. However, the 280 gallon limit forced the Offy to use 70 in-Hg boost. At this boost, the Offy produced 645 HP against 740 HP for the Cosworth. The reason for the relatively low fuel mileage of the Offy is that the air/fuel mix was about 20% richer (more fuel) than the Cosworth to prevent the engine from overheating. This was attributed to the lower piston area of the Offy.

# Chapter 23: Engine Life

### Reasons for Upgrading to a New Car

The vast majority of people replace their cars for social reasons rather than necessity.

1. Drive a later model car for prestige

2. Avoid high repair costs and in shop repair time by trading sooner than later

3. Take advantage of inherent higher reliability of a newer car

4. The newer interior will have fewer stains, less wear of the upholstery, no malfunctioning door or window controls, upgraded dashboard instruments and sound equipment, and no scratches or worn areas of the side panels, ceiling, and seat belts

Due to the inherent high depreciation of newer cars, many people drive their present cars longer and submit to higher repair costs and lower reliability. The major reasons for replacing these cars are far different than those as mentioned above.

1. Excessive oil consumption—failure to meet emission standards

2. Loss of power when climbing hills

3. Difficulty starting in cold weather

4.  Shifting discrepancies of automatic transmission

5.  Excessive engine noise—knocking, etc.

6.  Loss of engine oil pressure

## Maximum Engine Life—Primary Failure Mode of Engine

Assuming that the transmission will out last the engine, the question becomes, "What is the primary cause of engine failure?" This leads to a very old joke: If you ask 10 experts a question you will get 11 different answers. The following answers may be controversial, but can be indirectly proven by data gathered through experience with worn-out engines.

1.  Excessive wear of rings and cylinder walls

2.  Burned valves

3.  Excessive rod & main bearing wear

4.  Cracked block

Since the 1960s there have been improvements in engine design which have practically eliminated items 2, 3, and 4 above. Big improvements have been made in item 1. This item is considered to be the primary cause of engine failure.

Piston ring surfaces rely on metal to metal contact to seal the high combustion pressures from leaking to the crankcase, which causes loss of power. This inherent need for sealing prevents the use of smooth surfaces and reduced pressure to increase the life of the rings.

This same feature applies to the engine cylinder walls. Hardening the cylinder walls would reduce the ability to seal the combustion pressure.

## Factors Affecting Engine Life

A 1980s auto magazine article written by automotive engineers stated: "A car driven primarily on short trips—defined as 15 miles or less—will have 75% of all engine wear occur in the first three minutes of each trip."

The above statement will probably never be proven with scientific data; however, some tips on extending engine life may be indicated.

1.  If the coolant and oil temperatures could be maintained at operating temperatures while the car is parked, the wear should be reduced. This operation could be achieved in the owner's garage when the vehicle was not in use; the cost over the years would undoubtedly be greater than the cost of a replacement engine. Nothing feasible could be done when the vehicle is parked away from home.

2.  To provide rapid temperature rise, the engine should not be at idle during warm-up. As soon as the engine has started and is running smoothly, the car should be driven using partial throttle until the coolant is up to operating temperature.

3.  Short trips should be coordinated to reduce the time the vehicle is parked, even if the distance traveled is longer than normally required.

## Torque per Cubic Inch versus Engine Life.

Diesel engines are noted for their long life. The only diesel car engine studied was the 1978 Cadillac Seville Diesel. Although life figures were not available, it is estimated that 250,000 miles could be achieved with no major overhaul.

The displacement of the V8 is 349.892 cubic inches. The maximum torque was given at 220 lb-ft, which was confirmed with a vehicle performance analysis. Thus, $220 \div 349.892 = 0.6288$ lb-ft of torque per cubic inch.

A similar study of a 1984 Chevy Cavalier gave 108 lb-ft ÷ 121.503 cubic inch = 0.8889 lb-ft of torque per cubic inch. A detailed study of the Cavalier engine gave an estimated peak combustion pressure of 564 psi. Since the peak combustion pressure is approximately proportional to the torque per cubic inch, the maximum psi for the diesel is $\dfrac{0.6288 \times 564}{0.8889}$ = 399 psi.

Although life data for the Cavalier engine was not available, it is estimated that 150,000-175,000 miles could be achieved with no major overhaul. If engine life is inversely proportional to torque/cubic inch, then

$$\dfrac{399 \text{ psi (Diesel)}}{564 \text{ psi (Cavalier)}} = 0.7074$$

0.7074 x 250,000 miles (Diesel) = 176,862 miles (Cavalier).

This further tells us that devices used to increase torque/cubic inch (e.g., 4 valves/cylinder) will shorten engine life. The reason the auto makers go to higher torque/cubic inch without a major reduction in engine life is that the highway cruising speed uses a lower percentage of the maximum engine torque. Full throttle acceleration and hill-climbing will definitely reduce engine life.

If the teachings of the diesel engines were used, maximum torque/cubic inch would be limited to about 0.63 lb-ft per cubic inch, or 400 psi peak combustion pressure.

At 70 MPH Cavalier of 3330 lbs $WT_G$ requires
107.196 lb-ft x 0.57353 (efficiency) = 61.480 lb-ft
61.480 ÷ 121.503 in³ = 0.5060 lb-ft/in³
$\dfrac{0.5060 \times 564}{0.8889}$ = 321.1 psi

At 70 MPH Cadillac Diesel of 4490 lbs $WT_G$ requires

214.806 lb-ft x 0.6560551 (efficiency) = 140.925 lb-ft

140.925 ÷ 350.065 in³ = 0.402567 lb-ft/in³

$$\frac{0.402567 \times 564 = 255.4 \text{ psi}}{0.8889}$$

# Appendix One:
# #1 Test Vehicle

**1970 Honda CB750**

*Data Sheet: No. 3*       *Date: 12-01-1997*       *Rev: 3-1997*

Vehicle ID: 1970 Honda 750       $D_W$ = 25.887       (4:00-18)

| Gear | Ratio | $N_S$ | $V_S$ | M | $F_D$ | $F_D$ (Corr.) |
|------|-------|-------|-------|-----|--------|----------------|
| 1 | 2.5000 | 8552 | 47 | 12.9914 | 55.438 (.10) | |
| 2 | 1.7083 | 8455 | 68 | 8.8773 | 37.882 (.10) | |
| 3 | 1.3333 | 8539 | 88 | 6.9286 | 29.566 (.10) | |
| 4 | 1.0968 | 8462 | 106 | 5.6996 | 24.322 (.10) | |
| 5 | 0.9394 | 8426 | 123.24 | 4.8817 | 20.831 (.10) | |
| 6 | | | | | | |

| V | t-sec | V | t-sec |
|-----|-------|------|-------|
| 30 | 2.1 | 90 | 9.4 |
| 40 | 2.8 | 100 | 12.2 |
| 50 | 3.6 | 110 | 16.8 |
| 60 | 4.6 | 120 | |
| 70 | 5.8 | 130 | |
| 80 | 7.4 | 140 | |

$N_{(5)}$ 68.370659     $A_R$ 5.2654

Bore: 2.4016 inches     61.0 mm

Stroke: 2.480 inches     63.0 mm

Disp.: 44.9423 in³     736.46 cc

Power 65.0 (66) HP     8000 RPM

Torque 44.1 lb-ft     7000 RPM

$R_C$ 9.0     $N_L$ 12472 RPM

QM 13.35 sec @ 103.19 MPH     $E_V$ 0.7421 (0.8106)     $W_R$ 0.88267 (1.01005)

$WT_C$ 500 lbs     $WT_G$ 680 lbs     $F_R$ 19.72 lbs

| V | N | T | $F_M$ | $F_D$ | $F_A$ | $F_A$ @ 100 |
|--------|------|--------|---------|--------------|---------|-------------|
| 123.24 | 8426 | 40.147 | 195.988 | 19.599 (0.10) | 156.669 | 103.152 |
| Rider sitting up | | | | | | (+22.5) |
| 115.8 | 7917 | 42.900 | 209.423 | 22.942 (0.10) | 168.761 | 125.850 |
| | | | | | | |
| | | | | $F_T$ | $F_N$ | % grade |
| 65 | 4444 | 42.751 | 208.696 | 93.834 | 114.862 | 16.891 |
| | | | | | | |

$C_F$ = 0.0556591 x N (13.6)

| V | N | T | $F_M$ | $F_T$ | E | $C_F$ | MPG |
|----|------|--------|---------|--------|---------|--------------------------|-------|
| 65 | 4444 | 42.751 | 208.696 | 93.834 | 0.44962 | $\dfrac{1.1121317}{2.4734898}$ | 58.45 |

*Acceleration Times*                *Date: 12-1997*                *Rev: 3-1997*

Vehicle ID: 1970 Honda 750              No. 3

P = 65 @ 8000              T = 44.1 @ 7000      $F_A$ = 103.15 lbs @ 100 MPH

M (1) = 12.9914          $F_T$ (1) = 75.16 =(0.10)

M (2) = 8.8773           $F_T$ (2) = 57.60 = (0.10)

M (3) = 6.9286           $F_T$ (3) = 49.29 = (0.10)

M (4) = 5.6996           $F_T$ (4) = 44.04 = (0.10)          $\dfrac{KW}{G}$ =154.98

| V | N | T | $F_M$ | $F_A$ | $F_N$ | t |
|---|---|---|---|---|---|---|
| 0 | 0 | 0.85 / 37.485 | 486.98 | 0 | 411.82 | |
| 5 | ___ / 910 | 0.85 / 37.485 | 486.98 | 0.26 | 411.56 | 0.376 |
| 10 | ___ / 1820 | 0.85 / 37.485 | 486.98 | 1.03 | 410.79 | 0.377 |
| 15 | ___ / 2729 | 37.965 | 493.22 | 2.32 | 415.74 | 0.375 |
| 20 | 3639 | 41.251 | 535.91 | 4.13 | 456.62 | 0.355 |
| 25 | 4549 | 42.888 | 557.17 | 6.45 | 475.56 | 0.333 |
| 30 | 5459 | 43.701 | 567.73 | 9.28 | 483.29 | 0.323 |
| 35 | 6368 | 44.042 | 572.17 | 12.64 | 484.37 | 0.320 |
| 40 | 7278 | 43.990 | 571.49 | 16.50 | 479.83 | 0.321 |
| 45 | 8188 | 41.619 | 540.69 | 20.89 | 444.64 | 0.335 |
| 47 | 8552 / 5844 | 39.310 / 43.890 | 510.69 / 389.63 | 22.79 | 412.74 / 309.24 | 0.145} 0.447 |
| 50 | 6217 | 44.009 | 390.69 | 25.79 | 307.30 | 0.302} |
| 55 | 6838 | 44.096 | 391.46 | 31.20 | 302.66 | 0.508 |
| 60 | 7460 | 43.798 | 388.81 | 37.13 | 294.08 | 0.519 |
| 65 | 8082 | 42.225 | 374.85 | 43.58 | 273.67 | 0.546 |
| 68 | 8455 / 6599 | 39.958 / 44.078 | 354.72 / 305.40 | 47.70 | 249.42 / 208.41 | 0.356} 0.655 |
| 70 | 6793 | 44.094 | 305.51 | 50.54 | 205.68 | 0.299} |
| 75 | 7278 | 43.990 | 304.79 | 58.02 | 197.48 | 0.769 |
| 80 | 7763 | 43.269 | 299.79 | 66.02 | 184.48 | 0.811 |
| 85 | 8248 | 41.262 | 285.89 | 74.53 | 162.07 | 0.894 |
| 88 | 8539 / 7025 | 39.398 / 44.099 | 272.97 / 251.35 | 79.88 | 143.80 / 127.43 | 0.608}1.102 |
| 90 | 7184 | 44.052 | 251.08 | 83.55 | 123.49 | .494} |
| 95 | 7584 | 43.613 | 248.58 | 93.09 | 111.45 | 1.319 |
| 100 | 7983 | 42.721 | 243.49 | 103.15 | 96.30 | 1.492 |

### *Acceleration Times*

*Date: 12-1997*                    *Rev: 3-1997*

Vehicle ID: 1970 Honda 750                No. 3

$N_I=8$  $<N_T= 0.0017475$  $>N_T=0.014275$ (T)  $>N_P=0.032502$

P = 65 @ 8000                T=44.1 @ 7000                $F_A$= 103.15 lbs.

M (4) = 5.6996            $F_T$ (4) = 44.04 (0.10)

M (5) = 4.8817            $F_T$ (5) = 40.55 (0.10)

M ( ) =                $F_T$ ( ) =

M ( ) =                $F_T$ ( ) =                $\dfrac{KW}{G}$ =154.98

| V | N | T | $F_M$ | $F_A$ | $F_N$ | t |
|---|---|---|---|---|---|---|
| 100 | 7983 | 42.721 | 243.49 | 103.15 | 96.30 | |
| 105 | 8382 | 40.431 | 230.44 | 113.72 | 72.68 | 1.834 |
| 106 | 8462 / 7247 | 39.912 / 44.013 | 227.48 / 214.86 | 115.90 | 67.54 / 58.41 | 0.442} 2.772 |
| 110 | 7521 | 43.713 | 213.39 | 124.81 | 48.03 | 2.330} |
| 115 | 7863 | 43.037 | 210.09 | 136.42 | 33.12 | 3.820 |
| 118.24 | 8084 | 42.214 | 206.08 | 144.21 | 21.54 | 3.675 |
| 123.24 | 8426 | 40.147 | 195.99 | 156.67 | -0- | 14.390 |
| | | | | | | |
| | | | | | | |
| | | | | | | |
| | | | | | | |
| | | | | | | |
| | | | | | | |

$N_I=8$  $<N_T= 0.0017475$  $>N_T= 0.014275$ (T)  $>N_P= 0.032502$

$A_D$

*Date: 12-2-1997*                    *Rev: 2-1997*

Vehicle ID: 1970 Honda 750          No. 3

| V | $V_{FPS}$ | t | d | $d_t$ | $t_t$ |
|---|---|---|---|---|---|
| 5 | 3.666 | 0.376 | 1.4 | 1.4 | .376 |
| 10 | 11.000 | 0.377 | 4.1 | 5.5 | .753 |
| 15 | 18.333 | 0.375 | 6.9 | 12.4 | 1.128 |
| 20 | 25.666 | 0.355 | 9.1 | 21.5 | 1.483 |
| 25 | 33.000 | 0.333 | 11.0 | 32.5 | 1.816 |
| 30 | 40.333 | 0.323 | 13.0 | 45.5 | 2.139 |
| 35 | 47.666 | 0.320 | 15.3 | 60.8 | 2.459 |
| 40 | 55.000 | 0.321 | 17.7 | 78.4 | 2.780 |
| 45 | 62.333 | 0.335 | 20.9 | 99.3 | 3.115 |
| 50 | 69.666 | 0.447 | 31.1 | 130.5 | 3.562 |
| 55 | 77.000 | 0.508 | 39.1 | 169.6 | 4.070 |
| 60 | 84.333 | 0.519 | 43.8 | 213.3 | 4.589 |
| 65 | 91.666 | 0.546 | 50.0 | 263.4 | 5.135 |
| 70 | 99.000 | 0.655 | 64.8 | 328.2 | 5.790 |
| 75 | 106.333 | 0.769 | 81.8 | 410.0 | 6.559 |
| 80 | 113.666 | 0.811 | 92.2 | 502.2 | 7.370 |
| 85 | 121.000 | 0.894 | 108.2 | 610.4 | 8.264 |
| 90 | 128.333 | 1.102 | 141.4 | 751.8 | 9.366 |
| 95 | 135.666 | 1.319 | 178.9 | 930.7 | 10.685 |
| 100 | 143.000 | 1.492 | 213.4 | 1144.1 | 12.177 |

QM 13.35 sec @ 103.19 MPH

$A_D$    *Date: 12-2-1997*    *Rev: 2-1997*

Vehicle ID: 1970 Honda 750    No. 3

| $V$ | $V_{FPS}$ | $t$ | $d$ | $d_t$ | $t_t$ |
|---|---|---|---|---|---|
| 100 | 143.00 | 1.492 | 213.4 | 1144.1 | 12.177 |
| 105 | 150.333 | 1.834 | 275.7 | 1419.8 | 14.011 |
| 110 | 157.66 | 2.772 | 437.1 | 1856.8 | 16.783 |
| 115 | 165.000 | 3.820 | 630.3 | 2487.1 | 20.603 |
| 118.24 | 171.04266 | 3.675 | 628.6 | 3115.7 | 24.278 |
| 123.24 | 177.08533 | 14.390 | 2548.3 | 5663.9 | 38.668 |
|  |  |  |  |  |  |
|  |  |  |  |  |  |
|  |  |  |  |  |  |
|  |  |  |  |  |  |
|  |  |  |  |  |  |
|  |  |  |  |  |  |
|  |  |  |  |  |  |
|  |  |  |  |  |  |
|  |  |  |  |  |  |
|  |  |  |  |  |  |
|  |  |  |  |  |  |
|  |  |  |  |  |  |

QM 13.35 sec @ 103.19 MPH

# Appendix 2:
# #2 Test Vehicle

**1971 Toyota Corona Mark II**

*Data Sheet: No. 5*  *Date: 11-25-1990*  *Rev: 5-1984*

Vehicle ID: 1971 Toyota  $D_W = 23.50(.979)[5.50-13]$

| Gear | Ratio | $N_S$ | $V_S$ | M | $F_D$ | $F_D$ (Corr.) |
|------|-------|-------|-------|-----|-------|--------------|
| 1 | 3.658 | 6001 | 31 | 13.8226 | 293.125 | 483.656 (.33) |
| 2 | 2.119 | 5944 | 53 | 8.0071 | 169.800 | 237.720 (.28) |
| 3 | 1.403 | 5866 | 79 | 5.3015 | 112.425 | 129.288 (.23) |
| 4 | 1.000 | 5509 | 104.1 | 3.7787 | 80.132 | |
| 5 | | | | | | |
| 6 | | | | | | |

| V | t-sec | V | t-sec |
|-----|------|-----|------|
| 30 | 3.7 | 90 | 31.0 |
| 40 | 5.7 | 100 | |
| 50 | 8.0 | 110 | |
| 60 | 11.3 | 120 | |
| 70 | 15.2 | 130 | |
| 80 | 21.0 | 140 | |

$N_{(4)}$ 52.923421  $A_R$ 3.70

Bore: 3.386 inches  86.0 mm
Stroke: 3.150 inches  80.0 mm
Disp.: 113.458 in³  1858.82 cc
Power 107 (108) HP  5300 (5500) RPM
Torque 115 (117) lb-ft  3600 RPM
$R_C$ 9.0  $N_L$ 8049 RPM (55)

QM 18.38 sec @ 76.06 MPH  $E_V$ 0.76655 (0.83728)  $W_R$ 1.73023 (0.99604)
$WT_C$ 2310 lbs   $WT_G$ 2510 lbs   $F_R$ 72.79 lbs

| V | N | T | $F_M$ | $F_D$ | $F_A$ | $F_A$ @ 100 |
|---|---|---|-------|-------|-------|------------|
| 104.1 | 5509 | 101.419 | 383.231 | 76.646 | 233.795 | 215.741 |
| $W_T$ = 2680 (+370) | $F_R$ = 77.72 | | | | | |
| 103.5 | 5478 | 102.156 | 386.015 | 77.203 | 231.092 | 215.726 |
| | | | | | | |
| | | | | $F_T$ | $F_N$ | % grade |
| 73.0 | 3863 | 114.785 | 433.739 | 272.820 | 160.919 | 6.004 |
| | | | | | | |

$C_F = 0.1298646 \times N$ (15.2)

| V | N | T | $F_M$ | $F_T$ | E | $C_F$ | MPG |
|---|---|---|-------|-------|---|-------|-----|
| 70 | 3705 | 114.966 | 434.421 | 263.562 | 0.6067 | 2.9232 / 4.8182 | 23.95 |

*Acceleration Times*     *Date: 11-25-1990*          *Rev: 5-2-1984*

Vehicle ID: 1971 Toyota          No. 5

P = 107 @ 5300            T = 115 @ 3600          $F_A$ = 215.74 lbs

M (1) = 13.8226          $F_T$ (1) = 556.45 (0.33)

M (2) = 8.0071          $F_T$ (2) = 310.51 (0.28)

M (3) = 5.3015          $F_T$ (3) = 202.08 (0.23)

M (4) = 3.7787          $F_T$ (4) = 152.92 (0.20)          $\dfrac{KW}{G}$ = 572.07

| V | N | T | $F_M$ | $F_A$ | $F_N$ | t |
|---|---|---|---|---|---|---|
| 0 | 0 | 0.90 / 103.5 | 1430.64 | 0 | 874.19 | |
| 5 | 968 | 72.18 / 103.5 | 1430.64 | 0.54 | 873.65 | 0.655 |
| 10 | 1936 | 106.44 | 1471.31 | 2.16 | 912.70 | 0.640 |
| 15 | 2904 | 114.00 | 1575.80 | 4.85 | 1014.50 | 0.594 |
| 20 | 3872 | 114.77 | 1586.43 | 8.63 | 1021.35 | 0.562 |
| 25 | 4840 | 110.23 | 1523.64 | 13.48 | 953.71 | 0.579 |
| 30 | 5808 | 93.45 | 1291.76 | 19.42 | 715.89 | 0.685 |
| 31 | 6001 / 3476 | 87.56 / 114.97 | 1210.25 / 920.60 | 20.73 | 633.07 / 589.36 | 0.170} 0.952 |
| 35 | 3925 | 114.67 | 918.19 | 26.43 | 581.25 | 0.782} |
| 40 | 4486 | 112.56 | 901.31 | 34.52 | 556.28 | 1.006 |
| 45 | 5047 | 108.50 | 868.79 | 43.69 | 514.59 | 1.068 |
| 50 | 5607 | 98.98 | 792.51 | 53.94 | 428.06 | 1.214 |
| 53 | 5944 / 3935 | 89.35 / 114.65 | 715.47 / 607.83 | 60.60 | 344.36 / 345.15 | 0.889} 1.558 |
| 55 | 4084 | 114.27 | 605.82 | 65.26 | 338.48 | 0.669} |
| 60 | 4455 | 112.73 | 597.64 | 77.67 | 317.89 | 1.743 |
| 65 | 4826 | 110.34 | 584.94 | 91.15 | 291.71 | 1.877 |
| 70 | 5198 | 107.07 | 567.66 | 105.71 | 259.87 | 2.074 |
| 75 | 5569 | 99.94 | 529.85 | 121.35 | 206.42 | 2.454 |
| 79 | 5866 / 4181 | 91.74 / 113.95 | 486.35 / 430.59 | 134.64 | 134.64 / 143.03 | 2.571} 3.383 |
| 80 | 4234 | 113.75 | 429.84 | 138.07 | 138.85 | 0.812} |
| 85 | 4498 | 112.50 | 425.09 | 155.87 | 116.30 | 4.484 |
| 90 | 4763 | 110.80 | 418.69 | 174.75 | 91.02 | 5.519 |
| 95 | | | | | | |
| 100 | | | | | | |

$N_I$=5   <$N_T$= 0.0113925   >$N_T$= 0.0310348 (T)   >$N_P$= 0.1415906

*A*$_D$

**Vehicle ID: 1971 Toyota**

*Date: 11-25-1990*

No. 5

*Rev: 5-1984*

| V | V$_{FPS}$ | t | d | d$_t$ | t$_t$ |
|---|---|---|---|---|---|
| 5 | 3.666 | .655 | 2.4 | 2.4 | 0.655 |
| 10 | 11.000 | .640 | 7.0 | 9.4 | 1.295 |
| 15 | 18.333 | .594 | 10.9 | 20.3 | 1.889 |
| 20 | 25.666 | .562 | 14.4 | 34.8 | 2.451 |
| 25 | 33.000 | .579 | 19.1 | 53.9 | 3.030 |
| 30 | 40.333 | .685 | 27.6 | 81.5 | 3.715 |
| 35 | 47.666 | .952 | 45.4 | 126.9 | 4.667 |
| 40 | 55.000 | 1.006 | 55.3 | 182.2 | 5.673 |
| 45 | 62.333 | 1.068 | 66.6 | 248.8 | 6.741 |
| 50 | 69.666 | 1.214 | 84.6 | 333.3 | 7.955 |
| 55 | 77.000 | 1.558 | 120.0 | 453.3 | 9.513 |
| 60 | 84.333 | 1.743 | 147.0 | 600.3 | 11.256 |
| 65 | 91.666 | 1.877 | 172.1 | 772.4 | 13.133 |
| 70 | 99.000 | 2.074 | 205.3 | 977.7 | 15.207 |
| 75 | 106.333 | 2.454 | 260.9 | 1238.6 | 17.661 |
| 80 | 113.666 | 3.383 | 384.5 | 1623.1 | 21.044 |
| 85 | 121.000 | 4.484 | 542.6 | 2165.7 | 25.528 |
| 90 | 128.333 | 5.519 | 708.3 | 2874.0 | 31.047 |
| 95 | | | | | |
| 100 | | | | | |

QM 18.38 sec @ 76.06 MPH

# Appendix 3:
# #3 Test Vehicle

**1967 Chevrolet Bel Air**

*Data Sheet: No. 4*    *Date: 9-2-1990*    *Rev: 5-1984*

Vehicle ID: 1967 Chevrolet    $D_W = 26.00(.970)[8.00-14]$

| Gear | Ratio | $N_S$ | $V_S$ | M | $F_D$ | $F_D$ (Corr.) |
|------|-------|-------|-------|---|-------|---------------|
| 1 | 1.76 | 4587 | 60 | 5.4587 | 211.902 | 264.877 (.25) |
| 2 | 1.00 | 4691 | 108 | 3.1015 | 120.398 | |
| 3 | | | | | | |
| 4 | | | | | | |
| 5 | | | | | | |
| 6 | | | | | | |

| V | t-sec | V | t-sec |
|---|-------|---|-------|
| 30 | 5.2 | 90 | |
| 40 | 7.1 | 100 | |
| 50 | 9.3 | 110 | |
| 60 | 11.9 | 120 | |
| 70 | 16.4 | 130 | |
| 80 | 21.7 | 140 | |

$N_{(2)}$ 43.439016    $A_R$ 3.36

Bore: 3.875 inches    98.425 mm

Stroke: 3.000 inches    76.200 mm

Disp.: 283.038 in$^3$    4638.19 cc

Power 170 (195) HP    4600 (4800) RPM

Torque 245 (285) lb-ft    2900(2800) RPM

$R_C$ 9.25    $N_L$ 6878 (48) RPM

QM 19.34 sec @ 75.82 MPH    $E_V$ 0.66445 (0.72576)    $W_R$ 2.146903 (0.94366)

$WT_C$ 3675 lbs    $WT_G$ 3875 lbs    $F_R$ 112.375 lbs

| V | N | T | $F_M$ | $F_D$ | $F_A$ | $F_A$ @ 100 |
|---|---|---|-------|-------|-------|-------------|
| 108 | 4691 | 190.027 | 589.368 | 117.874 | 359.119 | 307.887 |
| $W_T = 4045$ (+370) | $F_R =$ 117.305 | | | | | |
| 107.6 | 4674 | 190.821 | 591.832 | 118.366 | 356.160 | 307.625 |
| | | | | $F_T$ | $F_N$ | % grade |
| 70 | 3041 | 243.174 | 754.205 | 388.563 | 365.642 | 9.039 |
| | | | | | | |

$C_F = 0.12667747 \times N$ (16.0)

| V | N | T | $F_M$ | $F_T$ | E | $C_F$ | MPG |
|---|---|---|-------|-------|---|-------|-----|
| 70 | 3041 | 243.174 | 754.205 | 388.563 | .5152 | $\frac{4.1796}{8.1126}$ | 16.75 |

**Torque Converter Data**     *Date: 9-2-1990*                    *Rev: 3-1997*
Vehicle ID: 1967 Chevrolet          No. 4

$M_1 = 5.4587$              $F_{D1} = 264.877 (0.25)$              $F_R = 112.375$

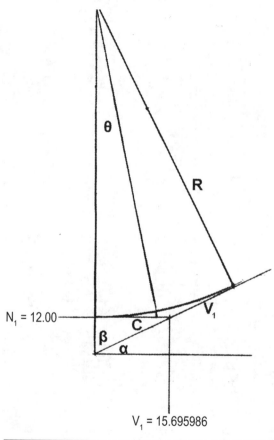

TC Ratio = 2.1

$\alpha = \text{inv tan } \dfrac{N_1}{V_1} = 37.398877°$

$\beta = 90° - \alpha = 52.601123$

$C = \dfrac{V_1}{\cos \alpha} = 19.757631$

$C + V_1 = 35.453617$

$R = [C + V_1] \tan \beta = 46.373289$

$\theta = \text{inv sin } \dfrac{V (5)}{R} = 6.189703$

$\Delta N = V (5) \tan \dfrac{\theta}{2} = 0.27$

$N_E = N_1 + \Delta N = 12.27$

$N_1 = 12.00$

$V_1 = 15.695986$

| V | $N_E$ | $N_S$ | $\Delta$ | .9 TCR MAX R | M | $F_D$ |
|---|---|---|---|---|---|---|
| 0 | 1200 | 0 | 1200 | 1.890 | 10.3169 | 500.618 |
| 5 | 1227 | 382 | 845 | 1.6267 | 8.8797 | 430.878 |
| 10 | 1309 | 765 | 544 | 1.4035 | 7.6611 | 371.746 |
| 15 | 1449 | 1147 | 302 | 1.2240 | 6.6814 | 324.205 |
| 20 | 1653 | 1529 | 124 | 1.0920 | 5.9607 | 289.237 |
| 25 | 1932 | 1911 | 21 | 1.0156 | 5.5437 | 269.002 |
| 30 | —— | 2294 | 0 | 1.0000 | 5.4587 | 264.877 |

**Acceleration Times**  Date: *11-25-1990*  Rev: *5-2-1984*

Vehicle ID: 1967 Chevrolet No. 4

P = 170 @ 4600  T = 245 @ 2900  $F_A$ = 307.89 lbs @ 100 MPH

M (1) = 5.4587  $F_T$ (1) = 377.25 (0.25

M (2) = 3.1015  $F_T$ (2) = 232.77 (0.20)

M (3) =  $F_T$ (3) =

M (4) =  $F_T$ (4) =  $\dfrac{KW}{G}$ = 883.18

| V | N | T | $F_M$ | $F_A$ | $F_N$ | t |
|---|---|---|---|---|---|---|
| 0 | 1100 / 0 | 182.358 | 1881.37 | 0 | 1268.38 | |
| 5 | 1227 / 382 | 196.487 | 1744.74 | 0.77 | 1200.72 | 0.715 |
| 10 | 1309 / 765 | 203.874 | 1561.90 | 3.08 | 1074.70 | 0.776 |
| 15 | 1449 / 1147 | 214.098 | 1430.48 | 6.93 | 986.97 | 0.857 |
| 20 | 1653 / 1529 | 224.993 | 1341.12 | 12.32 | 927.19 | 0.923 |
| 25 | 1932 / 1911 | 234.685 | 1301.02 | 19.24 | 900.40 | 0966 |
| 30 | 2294 | 241.595 | 1318.80 | 27.71 | 913.84 | .974 |
| 35 | 2676 | 244.600 | 1335.20 | 37.72 | 920.23 | .963 |
| 40 | 3058 | 242.91 | 1325.97 | 49.26 | 899.46 | .971 |
| 45 | 3440 | 234.87 | 1282.07 | 62.35 | 842.47 | 1.014 |
| 50 | 3823 | 223.58 | 1220.46 | 76.97 | 766.24 | 1.098 |
| 55 | 4205 | 209.99 | 1146.26 | 93.14 | 675.87 | 1.225 |
| 60 | 4587 / 2606 | 194.64 / 244.29 | 1062.50 / 757.68 | 110.84 | 574.41 / 414.07 | 1.413 |
| 65 | 2824 | 244.96 | 759.73 | 130.08 | 396.88 | 2.178 |
| 70 | 3041 | 243.17 | 754.20 | 150.86 | 370.57 | 2.302 |
| 75 | 3258 | 239.17 | 741.78 | 173.19 | 335.82 | 2.501 |
| 80 | 3475 | 233.95 | 725.61 | 197.05 | 295.79 | 2.797 |
| 85 | | | | | | |
| 90 | | | | | | |
| 95 | | | | | | |
| 100 | | | | | | |

$N_I$=5  $<N_T$= 0.0404938  $>N_T$= 0.1201322 (P)  $>N_P$= 0.3275982

$A_D$

*Date: 12-2-1997*                    *Rev: 2-1997*

Vehicle ID: 1967 Chevrolet              No. 4

| V | $V_{FPS}$ | t | d | $d_t$ | $t_t$ |
|---|---|---|---|---|---|
| 5 | 3.666 | .715 | 2.6 | 2.6 | .715 |
| 10 | 11.000 | .776 | 8.5 | 11.2 | 1.491 |
| 15 | 18.333 | .857 | 15.7 | 26.9 | 2.348 |
| 20 | 25.666 | .923 | 23.7 | 50.6 | 3.271 |
| 25 | 33.000 | .966 | 31.9 | 82.4 | 4.237 |
| 30 | 40.333 | .974 | 39.3 | 121.7 | 5.211 |
| 35 | 47.666 | .963 | 45.9 | 167.6 | 6.174 |
| 40 | 55.000 | .971 | 53.4 | 221.0 | 7.145 |
| 45 | 62.333 | 1.014 | 63.2 | 284.2 | 8.159 |
| 50 | 69.666 | 1.098 | 76.5 | 360.7 | 9.257 |
| 55 | 77.000 | 1.225 | 94.3 | 455.1 | 10.482 |
| 60 | 84.333 | 1.413 | 119.2 | 574.2 | 11.895 |
| 65 | 91.666 | 2.178 | 199.6 | 773.8 | 14.073 |
| 70 | 99.000 | 2.302 | 227.9 | 1001.7 | 16.375 |
| 75 | 106.333 | 2.501 | 265.9 | 1267.7 | 18.876 |
| 80 | 113.666 | 2.797 | 317.9 | 1585.6 | 21.673 |
| 85 | | | | | |
| 90 | | | | | |
| 95 | | | | | |
| 100 | | | | | |

QM 19.34 sec @ 75.82 MPH

# Appendix 4: Symbol Definitions

| | |
|---|---|
| $A_D$ | Acceleration page title—includes times, velocity and distance |
| A.F. | Alcohol fuel—methanol or ethanol |
| $A_F$ | Area—frontal (ft²) |
| $A_R$ | Axle ratio or final drive ratio |
| B | Bore—cylinder diameter (inches and/or millimeters) |
| Boost | Manifold pressure (in-Hg or psi) [1] |
| BSN | Bore times stroke times number of cylinders [2] |
| $C_D$ | Coefficient of aerodynamic drag |
| $C_f$ | Consumption of fuel (gal /hr) |
| $C_{Lf}$ | Coefficient of lift—front wheel |
| $C_{Lr}$ | Coefficient of lift—rear wheel |
| d | Distance traveled (feet) in the 5 or 10 MPH increments |
| $d_t$ (D) | Total distance traveled (feet) since start of acceleration |
| D | Displacement of engine  (in³ or cubic centimeters—cc) |
| $D_W$ | Diameter of drive wheel (inches) |
| E | Efficiency—total force needed divided by available force |

| $E_V$ | Efficiency—volumetric efficiency [3] |
|---|---|
| f | Fuel factor [4] |
| $F_A$ | Force—aerodynamic (lbs) |
| $F_C$ | Force—climbing |
| $F_D$ | Force—drive train |
| $F_M$ | Force maximum—gross |
| $F_N$ | Force net |
| $F_R$ | Force rolling resistance |
| $F_T$ | Force total |
| G | Gravitational acceleration: 32.174 ft/sec$^2$ |
| $WT_G$ | Gross vehicle weight |
| Hg | Mercury used in pressure measurements |
| HP | Horsepower |
| hr | Hours |
| I | Mass moment of inertia |
| K | Constant used in various formulas |
| M | Multiplier—when multiplied by torque, gives $F_M$ |
| MPG | Miles per gallon—fuel economy |
| MPH | Miles per hour |
| N | Number of revolutions per minute—RPM |
| $\Delta N$ | RPM difference between two specs |
| $N_C$ | RPM calculated |
| $N_E$ | RPM of engine |
| $N_I$ | RPM idle or stall |
| $N_L$ | Theoretical RPM where power drops to zero |
| $N_O$ | RPM of output shaft |
| $N_P$ | RPM where maximum power occurs |

| $N_S$ | RPM where transmission is shifted |
|---|---|
| $N_T$ | RPM where maximum torque occurs |
| $P$ | Power in horsepower (550 ft-lbs/sec) |
| $P_B$ | Pressure—barometric in inches of mercury (Hg) |
| $P_T$ | Power total |
| $Q_A$ | Flow of air/fuel mix |
| $Q_f$ | Flow of fuel |
| QM | Quarter mile—1320 feet—normal drag distance |
| $R_C$ | Ratio of compression |
| $\rho$ | Density of various fluids (weight/unit of volume) |
| $S$ | Stroke—total piston travel (inches and/or millimeters) |
| sec | Seconds |
| $SFC_G$ | Specific fuel consumption—gross [6] |
| $SFC_N$ | Specific fuel consumption—net [7] |
| t | Time (sec) to accelerate the 5 or 10 MPH increment |
| $t_t$ ($T_t$) | Time (sec) since the start of acceleration |
| $T$ | Torque in pound-feet (lb-ft) |
| TC | Torque converter |
| $T_A$ | Temperature of air—ambient (°F) |
| $T_B$ | Torque—base—for supercharged engine |
| $T_D$ | Torque drop from maximum torque RPM to maximum HP RPM |
| $T_L$ | Torque loss due to internal engine/accessory friction |
| $T_M$ | Torque maximum |
| $T_N$ | Torque net |
| $T_T$ | Torque—Total or gross—includes engine/accessory friction |
| $\mu$ | Coefficient of friction |
| $V$ | Velocity in MPH |

| $V_{fps}$ | Velocity in feet per second |
|---|---|
| $V_S$ | Velocity where transmission is shifted |
| $WT_C$ | Weight curb [8] |
| $WT_{G(T)}$ | Weight—gross or test (Gross vehicle weight—includes passengers, etc.) |
| $W_R$ | Weight reciprocating [9] |

### Notes

[1] Boost pressure in inches of mercury is usually absolute; the atmospheric pressure is included. Thus, 60 in Hg—29.98 in Hg (atmospheric)= 30.02 in/ Hg = 14.716 psi (gage pressure). Also; 24 psi (gauge) = 48.960 in-Hg + 29.98 (Atmospheric) = 78.940 in-Hg absolute.

[2] BSN is used to calculate internal engine friction. The final values are torque in lb-ft for the specific RPM listed.

[3] Volumetric efficiency is volume of air/fuel mix at atmospheric pressure and temperature taken during the engine intake stroke divided by the engine displacement.

[4] The fuel factor is the quantity of air/fuel mix for the type of fuel used including the air/fuel ratio required for the type of fuel being used.

[5] The multiplier is the primary drive ratio times the transmission ratio times the final drive ratio divided by the effective radius of the drive wheel in feet.

[6] Specific fuel consumption is usually given as net units of lbs of fuel per HP-hr. I use gallons of fuel per HP-hr and include the engine friction losses to enable the calculation of fuel consumption above the torque RPM.

[7] SFC. Net is similar to # 6 above without the internal engine friction losses. This can be used to compare fuel efficiency with other engines.

[8] Curb weight (lbs) of a vehicle includes all necessary fluids, one-half tank of fuel, but no passengers or cargo.

[9] Reciprocating weight for 1 cylinder (lbs) includes the entire piston, all rings, and wrist pin with keepers, and the shank of the connecting rod that extends beyond the nearly symmetrical bearing housing. The bearing housing and hardware (nuts, bolts, etc.) are considered rotating weight.

# About the Author

Roland Nelson is a native of San Jose, California, and received his B.S.M.E—Bachelor of Science Degree in Mechanical Engineering—from San Jose State University.

Although his entire career has been in the area of computer peripherals, his passion has been for the vehicles powered by internal combustion engines. By the 1980s, Nelson's analysis procedures were used to aid in selecting a new vehicle for purchase. Several analyses were made for friends and associates to aid them in selecting a vehicle for purchase.

After Nelson's retirement in 1996, he became a consultant to Sam Wheeler, the designer, builder, and rider of the E-Z-HOOK streamliner motorcycle for racing at the Bonneville salt flats. Wheeler set a new land speed record, sanctioned by the Southern California Timing Association (SCTA), of 332.410 MPH in August of 2004.

Nelson's second client, Mike Akatiff, contacted him in January 2003. The #899 streamliner motorcycle "Ack Attack" was completed in August of 2004, and set a land speed record for gasoline powered motorcycles of 328.304 MPH at Bonneville sanctioned by the SCTA.

Printed in the United States
by Baker & Taylor Publisher Services